SECOND EDITION

TOP NOTCH 3

Complete Assessment Package

with ExamView® Software

Joan Saslow • Allen Ascher

With Wendy Pratt Long and Penny Laporte

PEARSON
Longman

Top Notch: English for Today's World 3, Second Edition
Complete Assessment Package

with **ExamView** Assessment Suite CD-ROM

Copyright © 2011 by Pearson Education, Inc.
All rights reserved.

The tests in this publication are photocopiable. Pearson Education grants permission to classroom teachers to reproduce the tests for classroom use.

Pearson Education, 10 Bank Street, White Plains, NY 10606

Staff credits: The people who made up the *Top Notch 3 Complete Assessment Package, Second Edition* team—representing editorial, production, design, and manufacturing—are Jennifer Adamec, Rhea Banker, Diane Cipollone, Dave Dickey, Warren Fischbach, Aliza Greenblatt, Gosia Jaros-White, Mike Kemper, Pamela Kohn, Niki Lee, Barbara Sabella, and Martin Yu.

Cover Design: Rhea Banker
Cover Photo: Sprint/Corbis
Text composition: TSI Graphics
Text font: Palatino 11/12

ISBN 13: 978-0-13-247071-1
ISBN 10: 0-13-247071-3

Illustration credits: Steve Attoe, Deborah Crowle, Brian Hughes, Stephen Hutchings, Andy Meyer, Suzanne Mogensen, Dusan Petricic

Printed in the United States of America
2 3 4 5 6 7 8 9 10—V042—15 14 13 12 11

To The Teacher

The *Top Notch 3 Complete Assessment Package* contains the following photocopiable tests:

- An Achievement Test for each of the ten units in *Top Notch 3*
- Review Test 1 for Units 1–5
- Speaking Test 1 for Units 1–5
- Review Test 2 for Units 6–10
- Speaking Test 2 for Units 6–10

These tests are designed so that all students who have studied English using *Top Notch 3* have an opportunity to demonstrate their mastery of what they have studied.

Also included in this Complete Assessment Package are:

- The hybrid CD-ROM disk, which can be used as an audio CD or as a CD-ROM. As an audio CD, it is used to administer all the listening comprehension items in the Achievement Tests. As a CD-ROM, it is used to customize printable tests, using the **Exam**View® Assessment Suite product **Exam**View® Test Generator.* †
- An audioscript for the listening comprehension items.
- Answer keys for all tests.

ABOUT THE PRINTED TESTS IN THIS BOOKLET

ACHIEVEMENT TESTS

The Achievement Tests offer the opportunity to evaluate student progress on a unit-by-unit basis. Each Achievement Test is designed to be given upon completion of the corresponding unit in the Student's Book. Each Achievement Test contains 33 items and evaluates students' progress in:

- Listening
- Social language
- Vocabulary
- Grammar
- Reading
- Writing

REVIEW TESTS

The two Review Tests are cumulative tests. Review Test 1 is designed to be given after Units 1–5, and Review Test 2 after Units 6–10. Each Review Test contains 60 items that target the language taught throughout the previous five units. Like the Achievement Tests, the Review Tests begin with a listening section, which contains approximately 10 to 12 items. Each Review Test also contains 6 items of free writing.

SPEAKING TESTS

The Speaking Tests are cumulative tests of general speaking ability and are designed to be taken after Units 1–5 and Units 6–10. Each test contains 10 items that target the language taught in the corresponding units. The first 5 items relate to a detailed illustration, similar to the type of illustration on the last page of most units in the Student's Book. The last 5 items are personal questions related to topics from the units.

---

* **Exam**View® is a registered trademark of eInstruction Corp.

† **Exam**View is a software program that generates tests for you. You can use this program to create, customize, and print your own versions of *Top Notch* tests. (See page vii for a more complete description and instructions.)

Screenshot(s) reprinted by permission from eInstruction Corp.
Screenshots shown here may vary slightly.

▸ To The Teacher (continued)

ADMINISTERING THE PRINTED TESTS

ACHIEVEMENT TESTS AND REVIEW TESTS The listening comprehension items appear at the beginning of each test so that those items may be administered to all students at the same time. Play the correct track from the audio files of the hybrid CD-ROM disk and have students listen and answer the questions. Each listening exercise is recorded at least twice. The track number for each listening comprehension exercise is indicated above the audio icon on the page.

Each Achievement Test, including the listening comprehension section, is designed to take approximately 25 to 30 minutes to administer. Each Review Test requires approximately 50 minutes. Teachers may allow more or less time for any given test, depending on the needs of their students, without affecting the validity of the test.

SPEAKING TESTS Conduct Speaking Tests separately from Review Tests. Test students one at a time. Allow each student to study the illustration; then ask the questions. Before beginning the test, you may want to ask a few simple questions as a warm-up and to put your students at ease. For example, "Where is the woman? Point to her." "Where is the bank? Point to it." Each Speaking Test should take 3 to 5 minutes.

SCORING THE PRINTED TESTS

ACHIEVEMENT TESTS Each of the 33 items is worth 3 points for a total of 99 points. Count the number of correct items and multiply by 3. Allow 1 "free" point so that each test totals 100. The result will be a percentage score for each student.

REVIEW TESTS These tests have 60 items each, and each item is worth 1.5 points, for a total of 90 points.

SPEAKING TESTS The 10 items on each Speaking Test are worth 1 point each, for a total of 10 points. The Speaking Test and Review Test together equal 100 points.

SCORING RUBRICS FOR WRITING AND SPEAKING

The following criteria are offered to help evaluate students' responses in the free writing and speaking sections of the tests. The answer key contains model responses for each free writing item.

WRITING Use these criteria to evaluate student responses in any free writing sections of the tests.

> *Appropriate:* Responds to the question with a reasonable answer.
> *Complete:* Responds with a suitable amount of detail and uses varied vocabulary.
> *Accurate:* Response is clearly stated and grammatically correct.

On Achievement Tests (where each item is worth 3 points), give students 1 point for each criterion they meet. On Review Tests (where each item is worth 1.5 points), give students 0.5 point for each criterion they meet.

SPEAKING Use these criteria to evaluate student speaking skills in the Speaking Tests.

> *Appropriate:* Responds to the question with a reasonable answer.
> *Complete:* Responds with a suitable amount of detail and uses varied vocabulary.
> *Fluent:* Responds with ease and confidence; response flows smoothly and is not halting.
> *Intelligible:* Speaks clearly and can be readily understood by a native speaker.
> *Accurate:* Response is grammatically correct and uses colloquial expressions appropriately.

▶ To The Teacher (continued)

Use the following score sheet to help you evaluate each student's performance. Rate the student's response to each question on the test by checking the appropriate boxes on the score sheet. If a student's response is not "appropriate," do not check *any* boxes for that question. (A full-size reproducible version of the score sheet follows on the next page.)

	Appropriate	Complete	Fluent	Intelligible	Accurate	SCORE
Question 1	✓	✓	✓	✓	✓	5
Question 2	✓		✓		✓	3
Question 3						0
Question 4	✓	✓	✓		✓	4
Question 5	✓		✓	✓	✓	4
Question 6	✓	✓	✓			3
Question 7	✓	✓		✓		3
Question 8	✓		✓		✓	3
Question 9	✓	✓			✓	3
Question 10	✓	✓				2

TOTAL ___30___

Write the number of checks, and then total them. Award points as shown below.

Score	Total points		Score	Total points
46–50	10		21–25	5
41–45	9		16–20	4
36–40	8		11–15	3
31–35	7		6–10	2
26–30	6		1–5	1

ABOUT EXAM*VIEW*

Exam*View* software contains a question bank of items for each *Top Notch* unit and review test. The question bank includes all the items from the photocopiable tests PLUS several new items.

Exam*View* allows you to do the following:

- Select the test items that are best for your class
- Edit test items to change names, places, words, etc.
- Create your OWN original test items

The tests you create with **Exam***View* can be printed on paper or delivered electronically (online or LAN-based).

INSTALLING EXAM*VIEW*

Before installing **Exam***View*, please verify that your computer meets the system requirements specified on the last page of this booklet.

These instructions are for the Release 6 version. If you have an earlier version of **Exam***View* installed on your computer, it will be automatically replaced by this version upon installation. You can then create all your new tests in this version. If you open an existing test or question bank from the earlier version, it will be automatically updated.

Speaking Test Score Sheet

Response is . . .

	Appropriate	Complete	Fluent	Intelligible	Accurate	SCORE
Question 1						
Question 2						
Question 3						
Question 4						
Question 5						
Question 6						
Question 7						
Question 8						
Question 9						
Question 10						

TOTAL _____

Student _____

➡ **To The Teacher** (continued)

For Windows®:

1. Close all other programs before you begin the installation.
2. Insert the **Exam***View* disk into the CD-ROM drive of your computer.
3. You may be prompted by the computer to open the disk. If not, open **My Computer**.
4. Double-click on the CD-ROM drive icon.
5. Double-click on the **SETUP** file and follow the instructions on the screen.
6. When installation is complete, remove the **Exam***View* disk from the CD-ROM drive of your computer.

For Macintosh®:

1. Close all other programs before you begin the installation.
2. Insert the **Exam***View* disk into the CD-ROM drive of your computer.
3. Double-click on the **Exam***View* disk icon on the desktop.
4. Double-click on the **Exam***View* installer icon and follow the instructions on screen.
5. When installation is complete, remove the **Exam***View* disk from the CD-ROM drive of your computer.

PRODUCT SUPPORT

For technical support, we recommend e-mailing EPSupport@pearson.com or calling us. Within the United States, dial 1-877-546-5408. Outside the United States, dial +1-914-287-8980.

Please have the following information ready when you contact technical support:

- the product title and ISBN (for example, *Top Notch 3*, ISBN 0-13-247071-3)
- computer type and operating system (for example, Windows or Mac; Which version?)
- a detailed description of the problem, including any error messages you received

OPENING EXAM*VIEW*

Once **Exam***View* is installed, double-click on the **Exam***View* **Test Generator** icon on your desktop. If there is no icon, open the **Start** menu. Click on **Programs**. Click on **Exam***View* **Pro Test Generator**. Click on **Exam***View* **Test Generator**. On a Mac, click on the **Exam***View* **Test Generator** icon in the dock. If you do not see this icon, locate the **Exam***View* **Pro** folder on your hard drive. Double-click on the **Exam***View* **Test Generator** icon.

If you have not registered your copy of **Exam***View*, you might be asked to register the software. You can register at any time. After exiting registration, you will see the **Exam***View* **Test Generator** menu. All of our instructions will start from this menu.

RECOMMENDED SETTINGS FOR *TOP NOTCH*

We recommend the following procedure to ensure that your **Exam***View* tests for *Top Notch* display optimally. These settings will be permanent.

▶ **To The Teacher** (continued)

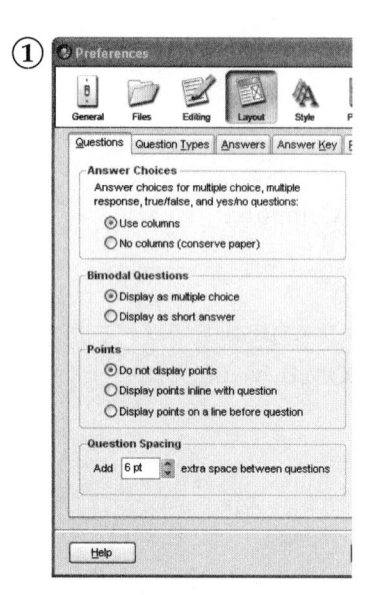

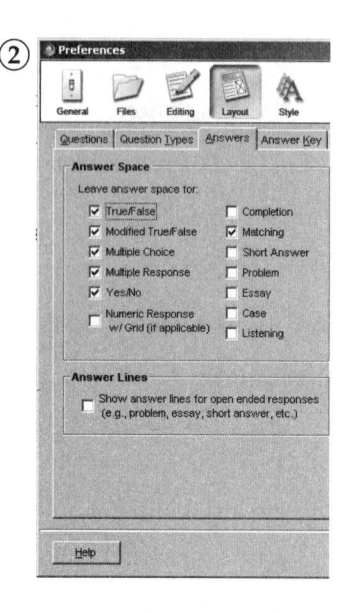

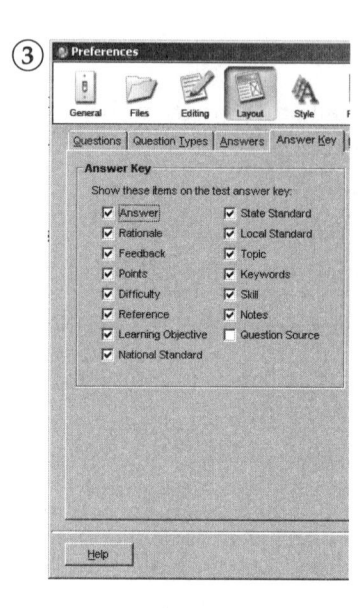

Click on **Close** in the **ExamView Test Generator** menu. Click on **Edit** from the top of the **ExamView Test Builder** window and select **Preferences** from the drop-down menu. You will see the **Preferences** screen. Select **Layout**. Set all of the checkboxes under the **Questions** tab to match screenshot ①. Select the **Answers** tab. Set all of the checkboxes to match screenshot ②. Select the **Answer Key** tab. Set all of the checkboxes to match screenshot ③. Click on the **Save as Default** button at the bottom of your screen to make these changes permanent.

The *Top Notch Complete Assessment Package* tests have customized instructions and examples for each exercise. Because **ExamView** provides its <u>own</u> instructions, BOTH will appear in your customized tests unless you take the following steps to remove the **ExamView** instructions.

Choose **Test** from the **ExamView Test Builder** window and select **Instructions** from the drop-down menu. You will see a list of the available question types. Select each of the question types listed at the end of this paragraph and delete the default instruction. Do not delete the question type header. For example, select the **True/False** question type. Delete the instruction "Indicate whether the statement is true or false." Do not delete the header True/False. Then click on the **Save As Default** button in order to make this change permanent. Repeat this step for each of the following question types: **True/False, Modified True/False, Multiple Choice, Multiple Response, Yes/No,** and **Completion**.

CREATING TESTS WITH EXAMVIEW

All of the following instructions start from the **ExamView Test Generator** menu. This menu is presented when you open the **ExamView** Test Generator software. At any point, you can go to this menu by closing and opening the **ExamView** Test Generator software.

CREATING A NEW TEST

There are two ways to select test items to create a new test: "Create a new test from scratch" or "Create a new test using a wizard." It is strongly recommended that you select "Create a new test from scratch" because you will get better results.

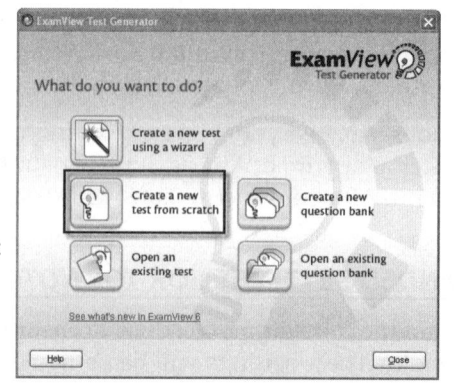

Click on "Create a new test from scratch." Name your test in the space provided and click on **OK**. Click on **OK** again to exit the **Information** window. You will now see a blank test page with a name and date line at the top.

→ **To The Teacher** (continued)

USING "SELECT ALL"

On the toolbar, click on the **Select All** icon.

Next, you will see this window, which shows the available question banks.

The question banks are organized by *Top Notch* unit and review test. Highlight a unit you want to include on your test. Click on **Select**. Repeat this for any additional unit you wish to include. When you have all the units you want, click on **OK**. Then click on **Yes** (or **Select** on a Mac) in the pop-up window.

Your test now includes all the available items. You can now customize your test.

Note: It is recommended that you always use **Select All** to create your test. While other selection methods are available (described below), they don't work optimally with the rich variety of language skills included in the *Top Notch* question banks.

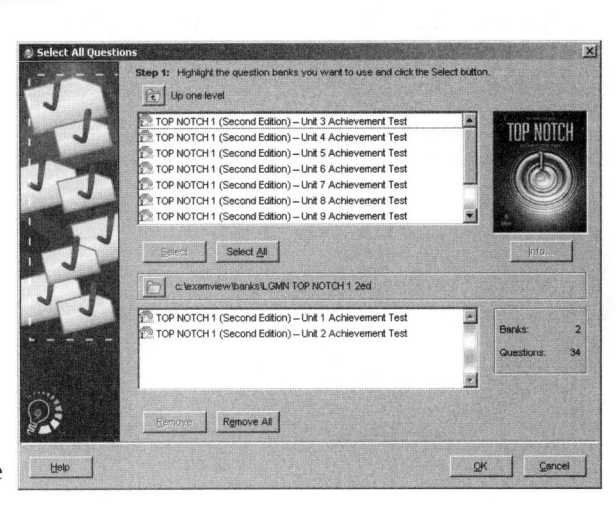

CUSTOMIZING YOUR TEST

You can now delete, edit, or create new items.

DELETING ITEMS YOU DON'T WANT

Highlight the item you wish to delete. Click on the **Delete** button at the bottom of the screen. Then click on **Yes** (or **Remove** on a Mac) in the pop-up window. Repeat this step for each item you wish to delete.

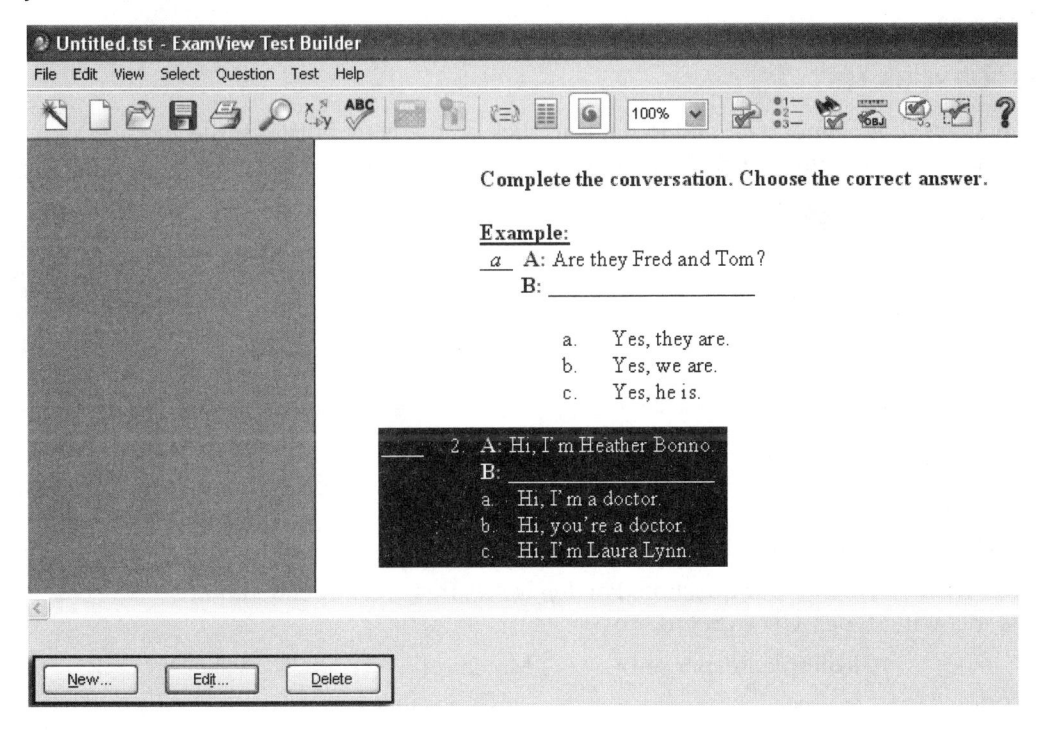

If you wish to delete artwork in test items, you may select it and delete it. You can also replace artwork in the test items by pasting another illustration into the test.

→ **To The Teacher** (continued)

EDITING ITEMS (AND INSTRUCTIONS) YOU WISH TO CHANGE

Highlight the item or the instructions you wish to change. Click on the **Edit** button at the bottom of the screen as shown in the previous screen. You will now see a screen that looks like this:

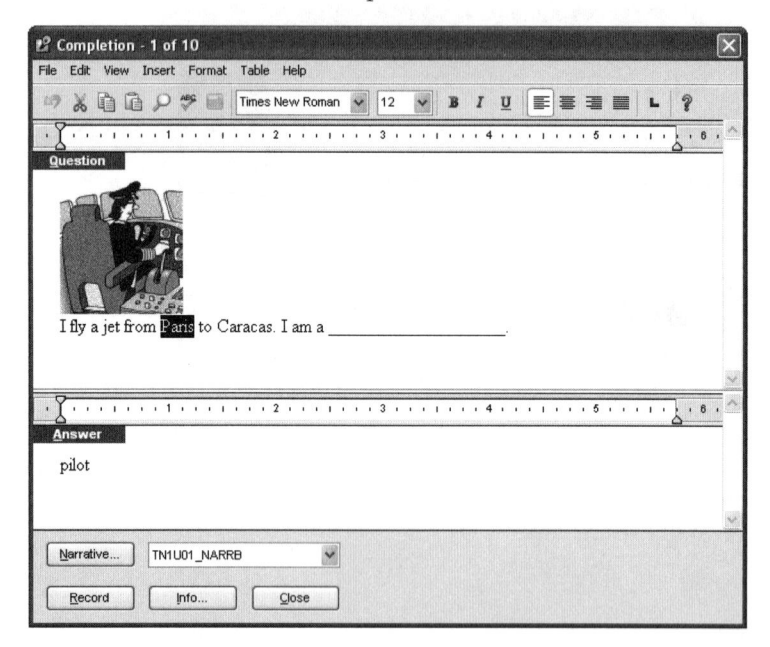

Highlight any word or words within the **Question** field (the top half of the screen) and edit the item in the same manner as you would on a word processor. (For example, "Paris" could be changed to any other city.) Be sure to edit the answer in the **Answer** field (the bottom half of the screen) as appropriate.

Click on the **Record** button at the bottom of the screen. Your edited item will now appear on your customized test. If you wish to change the instructions, highlight them and edit them in the same way as you edit an item.

WRITING NEW ITEMS FOR YOUR TEST

If you want to write new items that are not included in the test, click on the **New** button at the bottom of the screen (shown in the Deleting Items section, p. ix). You will now see this screen:

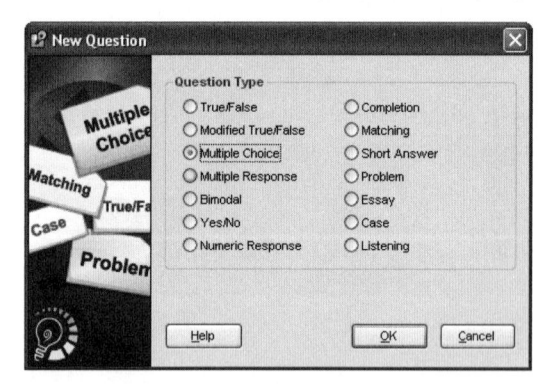

Choose the item type you wish to use for your question. For *Top Notch*, it is recommended that you select only from the following types. Click on **OK**.

True/False	Multiple Response	Matching
Modified True/False	Yes/No	Short Answer
Multiple Choice	Completion	Essay

▶ To The Teacher (continued)

Follow the instructions to create and record (save) your item. Repeat these steps for each new item you wish to write.

Note: Your new items will appear with other items of the same type; for instance, if you write a multiple choice item, it will appear with all other multiple choice items already on the test.

ADDING NEW READING AND LISTENING QUESTIONS

In **Exam***View*, each reading and listening section has been treated as a single "item" in order to protect the integrity of the *Top Notch* tests. Choose Listening or Problem only if you wish to create a listening or reading section. (The item type "Problem" refers to a reading section.)

To add a new listening or reading question, highlight the reading or listening section you wish to change. Click on the **Edit** button at the bottom of the screen. Type in a new question. (You may need to renumber items as appropriate.) Click on the **Record** button.

Note: If you decide to edit, delete, or add items to the listening section, the item numbers may not match what students hear on the audio (because these have been recorded to correspond to the ready-made printed tests in the booklet).

SAVING, PRINTING, AND CLOSING YOUR TEST

To save your test, click on the **Save** icon on the toolbar.

To print your test, click on the **Print** icon on the toolbar.

To close your test, go to the **File** menu and click on **Close**.

OTHER WAYS TO CREATE TESTS USING EXAM*VIEW*

USING "SELECT WHILE VIEWING"

Click on the **Select While Viewing** icon. Then select the question banks the same way you did for **Select All**, and click on **Next** when you're done. Now the computer will show you all the questions from the question banks you selected. Check and/or double-click on the items you wish to include in your test.

When you're done, click on **Finish** at the bottom of the screen. You may now edit items or add your own items as described above.

USING "SELECT BY STANDARD"

This option lets you choose items by *Top Notch* learning objectives.
Click on the **Select By Standard** icon. Next, select your question banks. Click on **Next**.

Exam*View* lists the grammar learning objectives for the question banks you chose. In the "Additional Selections" column, type in the number of items for each learning objective you wish to include. When finished, click on **Select** at the bottom of the screen and then **Close**.

USING "SELECT BY CRITERIA"

This option lets you choose items by various categories. Click on the **Select By Criteria** icon. Next, select your question banks. Click on **Next**. You can choose any combination of the following fields: Difficulty, Reference, Learning objective, and Skill. (See screenshot on next page.) Do this by selecting the icon to the right of the criteria you wish to include and choosing the value you want. (See screenshot on next page.) When you have finished, click on **Select While Viewing** at the bottom of the screen. Check and/or double-click on the items you wish to include in your test. Click on **OK** and then **Close**.

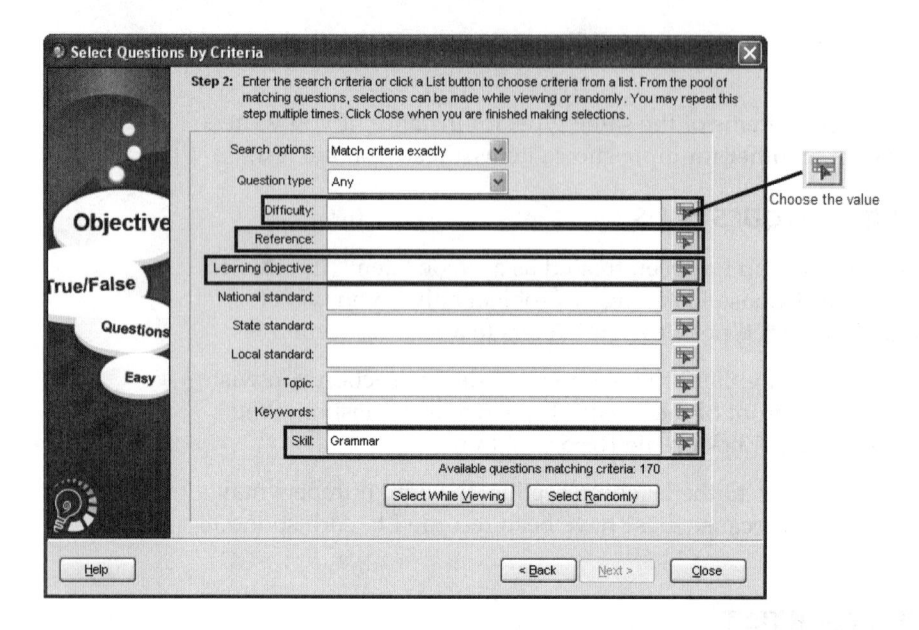

▶ To The Teacher (continued)

USING "SELECT RANDOMLY" AND "SELECT FROM A LIST"

Note: These selection methods are not recommended for *Top Notch*.

USING THE "QUICKTEST WIZARD"

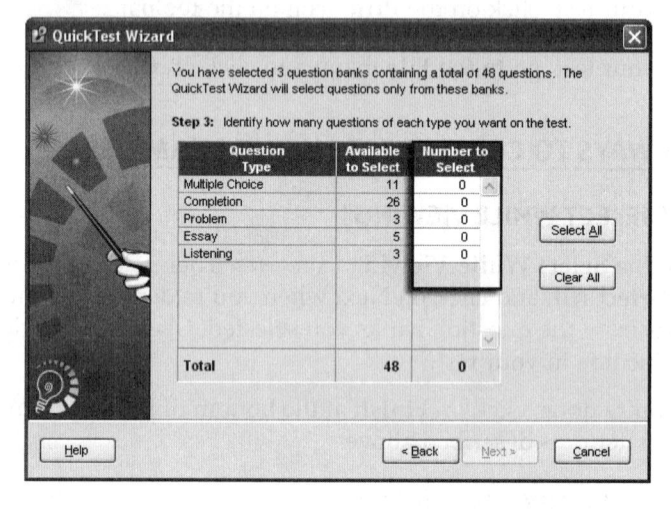

From the **Exam*View* Test Generator** menu, click on "Create a new test using a wizard." Next, give your test a name in the space provided. Click on **Next**. In the next screen, choose the question banks. Click on **Next**, and you will then see this screen:

Enter the number of items you wish to select. Then click on **Next**.

Note: The *QuickTest Wizard* is a fast way to create a ready-made test by item type. However, because the *Top Notch* tests contain a variety of media and skill types, the number of items indicated on the menu doesn't accurately indicate the actual number of items available for each unit. For example, each listening section and each reading section is treated as a single "item" in **Exam*View*** ("Listening" and "Problem"). The number in "Available to Select" does not reflect the actual number of listening and reading items. For those question types, select all "available" items and then delete those you don't want when you open your test.

OPENING AN EXISTING TEST

To open a test you have already created and saved, click on the "Open an existing test" option in the **Exam*View* Test Generator** menu. You may now modify or print this test using the procedures described above.

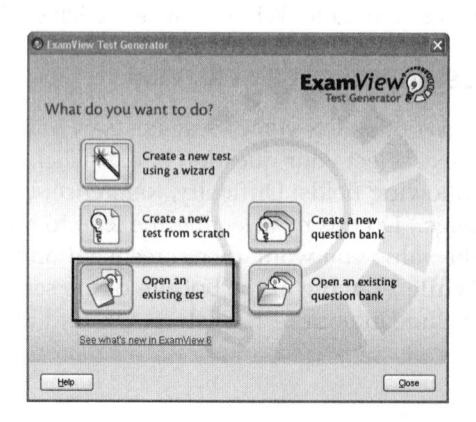

UNIT 1 Achievement Test

Name _____

Track 02
🔊 **Listen to the conversations. Read the sentences. Then listen again and circle the word or phrase that correctly completes each sentence.**

Example: The woman prefers to be called (Mrs. / Miss /(Ms.)) Graham.

1. It is (**impolite / taboo / customary**) to use first names at this office.
2. Ayako registered for the conference (**before / after / when**) it was announced.
3. In Sophia's culture it's (**bad table manners / taboo / impolite**) to eat beef.
4. The man would like to be called by his (**first name / title and last name / title and first name**).
5. They are talking about (**table manners / greetings / punctuality**).
6. First, Ms. Pilman (**taught a class / became a doctor / went to her doctor**).
7. In Patricia's culture, it's (**offensive / good etiquette / customary behavior**) for a student to use a teacher's first name.

Complete each sentence with a word or phrase from the box. You will not use all of the words.

customary	etiquette	impolite	punctuality
~~small talk~~	table manners	taboo	

Example: It's appropriate to make _____small talk_____ when you first meet a person.

8. If something is _____ in a culture, it is not allowed.
9. The _____ traditions are what people usually do.
10. It's important to have good _____ when you eat with other people.
11. Different cultures have different rules about _____, or what is considered polite.

Complete each statement with a tag question.

Example: She was in Thailand last semester, _____wasn't she_____?

12. You're going to New Zealand, _____?
13. I'm not enrolled in the class yet, _____?
14. Dr. Holland prefers to be called Michael, _____?
15. They have contacted the director of the program, _____?
16. Your parents didn't grow up in Madrid, _____?

1

UNIT 1 — Achievement Test (continued) Name _____

Read each sentence. Then write a number <u>1</u> next to the event that happened first, and a number <u>2</u> next to the event that happened second.

<u>Example:</u> I'd already made plans with Patrick when you told me about the party.
  __1__ I made plans with Patrick.   __2__ You told me about the party.

17. By the time she left Spain, she'd learned Spanish pretty well.
  _____ She left Spain.   _____ She learned Spanish pretty well.

18. He had already heard the news when his boss told him about the promotion.
  _____ He heard the news.   _____ His boss told him about the promotion.

19. When we arrived at the office, the meeting had started.
  _____ We arrived at the office.   _____ The meeting started.

Look at some of Laura's life events. Complete each statement, using the past perfect and <u>already</u> or <u>yet</u>. Use contractions when possible.

Timeline:
- 1996: got her first job
- 1997: bought a new car
- 1998: traveled to London with friends
- 1999: began Japanese language classes
- 2000: got married
- 2001: moved to Chicago
- 2002: found a new job
- 2003: started business school
- 2004: bought a house
- 2005: went to Japan on vacation

<u>Example:</u> By 2001, Laura had already gotten married, but she __hadn't yet found__ a new job.

20. Laura _____ a house when she bought a new car.
21. By the time she went to Japan on vacation, Laura _____ Japanese language classes.
22. By 2004, Laura _____ business school.

Match each sentence on the left to the one on the right with the most similar meaning. Write the letter.

<u>Example:</u> Please call me Ann. __b__

23. Do you mind if I call you by your first name? _____
24. What would you like to be called? _____
25. Should I use your title? _____

a. How do you prefer to be addressed?
b. We're on a first-name basis here.
c. Do you want to be addressed as Doctor?
d. Would it be rude to call you John?

Read the article. Then read it again and check true or false.

The Culture of Fashion

Imagine someone getting dressed. This person puts on a wig of long, curly hair, clothes decorated with gold, jewels, and ribbons, and then high-heeled shoes. Who is this woman? Well, the year is 1683, and the person isn't a woman at all. It is King Louis XIV of France!

Fashion is a part of culture that has changed a lot over time. Wigs and high-heeled shoes certainly aren't popular for men anymore. So specific fashions have changed, but what about the *culture* of fashion?

The *culture* of fashion refers to how certain styles become popular at certain times. Throughout history, people have modeled their clothing after famous people. In the 1600s, people imitated the styles of kings and queens. Nowadays, people want to look like movie stars. The culture of fashion has remained the same, though: People still follow the trends of the rich and famous.

Nearly everyone is influenced by fashion. Even if you don't know the names of any top designers, you probably know what new styles people are wearing. This is fashion.

Fashion has changed with the times, but the culture of fashion really hasn't changed a lot over time. People still tend to dress like the people around them, choosing types of clothing that are most popular at the moment.

SOURCE: encarta.msn.com

		true	false
Example:	King Louis XIV of France was a woman.	☐	☑
26.	Fashion changes with time.	☐	☐
27.	Fashion wasn't part of culture in the past.	☐	☐
28.	You can know about fashion without knowing the names of designers.	☐	☐
29.	The culture of fashion has changed a lot over time.	☐	☐
30.	People often wear clothes that are similar to other people's.	☐	☐

UNIT 1 — Achievement Test (continued) Name _____

Choose one of the following topics to write about. Write four or five sentences.

- Think about an extremely busy day, morning, week, or other period of time in your recent experience. Why was it so busy? What had you done by the end of the time period? Use the past perfect and <u>already</u> or <u>yet</u> in some of your sentences.
- Discuss etiquette in your country. Use words from the box and your own words.

| cultural literacy | customary | etiquette | impolite |
| offensive | punctuality | table manners | taboo |

31–33. _____

UNIT 2 Achievement Test

Name _____

Track 03

🔊 **Listen to the conversations. Look at the pictures. Then listen again and write the letter of the picture that matches each conversation.**

Example: __b__

1. _____
2. _____
3. _____

a.

b.

c.

d.

Track 03

🔊 **Listen to the conversation. Read the sentences. Then listen again and check <u>true</u> or <u>false</u>.**

	true	false
Example: The patient has an emergency.	✔	☐
4. The dentist thinks the patient isn't in a lot of pain.	☐	☐
5. It's impossible for the dentist to fix the tooth today.	☐	☐
6. The dentist might give the patient some medication.	☐	☐

1

UNIT 2 — Achievement Test (continued) Name _____

Look at the pictures. Write the medication that is best for each symptom. Use words from the box. You will not use all of the words.

| antacid | ~~antihistamine~~ | cough medicine |
| ointment | painkiller | |

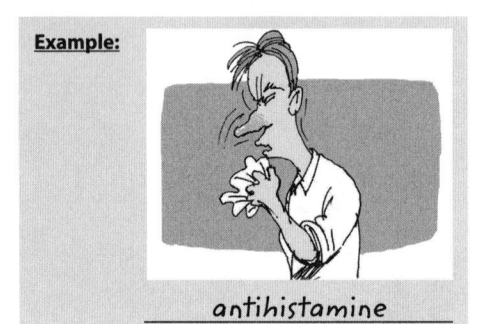

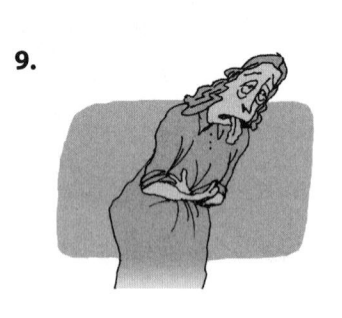

Example: ___antihistamine___

7. _____

8. _____

9. _____

Complete each conversation with <u>may</u>, <u>might</u>, or <u>must</u>. Some sentences have more than one possible answer.

Example: **A:** Hi. I wonder if I might be able to see the dentist?
B: I'll have to check. He ___might___ have time after lunch.

10. **A:** Anna's not at work today.
    B: She _____ be really sick because she never misses work.

11. **A:** Can I get an appointment with the doctor today?
    B: I don't know. She _____ be too busy.

12. **A:** The children were so sick yesterday. Do they feel better today?
    B: They _____ feel better because they're outside playing.

13. **A:** I feel terrible. Do you think I should go to the doctor?
    B: Maybe. You _____ have something serious.

UNIT 2 — Achievement Test (continued) Name _____

Read the sentences. Then check the statement that is closer in meaning to the original sentence.

> **Example:** My back really hurts.
> ☑ I have a lot of back pain.   ☐ My back might be bothering me.

14. Kelly is very nauseous.
    ☐ She feels like she's going to vomit.   ☐ She feels like she can't breathe.

15. Thanks for fitting me in.
    ☐ Thanks for giving me an appointment.   ☐ Thanks for making me feel better.

16. I'm sick and it's an emergency.
    ☐ I'll take something later if I don't feel better.   ☐ I need help immediately.

17. Nausea is a side effect of the medication.
    ☐ The medication is for nausea.   ☐ The medication can make you feel nauseous.

Complete each sentence. Circle the letter of the correct answer.

> **Example:** If you have a cold, you might feel _____.
> (a.) weak   b. a pain in your hip   c. like your gums are swollen

18. You should go to the doctor for _____ to make sure you are healthy.
    a. a prescription   b. a checkup   c. an antihistamine

19. If you want a prescription for medication, you should go to _____.
    a. a conventional doctor   b. an acupuncturist   c. a spiritual healer

20. I need to see a dentist because _____.
    a. my gums are swollen   b. I have a high fever   c. I'm dizzy

21. If you have a pain in your leg, you might need _____.
    a. a decongestant   b. an X-ray   c. an EKG

22. _____ uses the mind or religious faith to treat illness.
    a. Herbal therapy   b. Acupuncture   c. Spiritual healing

UNIT 2 — Achievement Test (continued) Name _____

Complete each conversation in your own way. Make conclusions with must.

> **Example:** "I've had a headache for two days."
>
> (YOU) _____ You must feel awful! _____

23. "My eyes are red and itchy, and I can't stop sneezing."

    (YOU) _____

24. "Susie broke her tooth last night during dinner."

    (YOU) _____

25. "I just won $1,000!"

    (YOU) _____

Read the article. Then read it again and check the true statement for each item.

Laughter Is the Best Medicine

There's a saying in English: "Laughter is the best medicine." Now studies suggest that this saying might really be true.

Everyone knows that stress is bad for your health. It can give you headaches. It can cause heart attacks and other serious medical problems. When we laugh, our stress is reduced. Then the body is able to fight disease better.

People who laugh a lot have lower blood pressure than the average person. When a person laughs, his or her blood pressure goes down. When this happens, breathing becomes deeper, sending more oxygen and nutrients throughout the body. Also, laughter pushes out more air from the lungs than it takes in, which helps to clean out the lungs.

Laughter is good exercise, too! Some doctors have estimated that a person can burn as many calories by laughing as by riding an exercise bike for several minutes.

Laughter can even help improve your memory. When you laugh, your muscles relax and psychological stress is reduced. This keeps the brain alert and allows you to remember more information.

Some doctors are beginning to prescribe laughter along with certain medications and a healthy diet. It's easy to include laughter in your daily schedule. Just read something humorous or watch a funny video. And who knows— it might save your life!

Example: ☑ Laughter can help reduce stress.
☐ When you laugh, you can't have any stress.

26. ☐ Laughter can give you headaches.
    ☐ Laughter can help your body fight disease.

27. ☐ Laughter can cause high blood pressure.
    ☐ If you need to lower your blood pressure, laughing might help.

28. ☐ It's better for your health to laugh than to ride an exercise bike.
    ☐ Laughter is one form of exercise.

29. ☐ You will remember things better if you laugh after you learn them.
    ☐ Laughing keeps your brain healthy so you can remember more.

30. ☐ Laughter is better than medicine.
    ☐ Laughter is one good way to improve your health.

UNIT 2 — Achievement Test (continued) Name _____

Choose one of the following topics to write about. Write four or five sentences.

- Think about one type of medical treatment (conventional medicine, homeopathy, herbal therapy, acupuncture, or spiritual healing). What do you like and/or dislike about this treatment? Why?

- Create a conversation for one of the following situations:

    1. You ask a friend to recommend a doctor.
    2. You call the receptionist to make an appointment.
    3. You arrive at the office and are greeted by the receptionist.
    4. The doctor asks you about the problem and suggests a treatment.

31–33. _____

_____

_____

_____

_____

_____

_____

_____

UNIT 3 Achievement Test

Name _____

Track 04

🔊 **Listen to the conversation. Look at the chart. Then listen again and complete the chart. Use words from the box. You will not use all of the words.**

| auto repair | copying | fast | helpful | ~~housecleaning~~ |
| printing | professional | reasonable | reliable | tailoring |

Name of business	Kind of service	Adjective to describe service
Maid to Clean	**Example:** housecleaning	1.
Edison's	2.	3.
Tony's	4.	5.
Sew Good	6.	7.

Complete each sentence with the correct form of the verb in parentheses.

Example: I'd like to have this invitation ___printed___, please.
(print)

8. My mom made me _____ to the store with her, even though I didn't want to.
(go)

9. You can have the chef _____ the menu, or you can choose your own food.
(plan)

10. If you get that picture _____, it'll look a lot better.
(frame)

11. Who can get the job _____ on time?
(finish)

12. The shoe repair place lost Bill's shoes, so he made them _____ for a new pair.
(pay)

1

UNIT 3 — Achievement Test (continued) Name _____

Write the words and phrases in the correct order.

> **Example:** his assistant / copy / have / a few extra pages / He'll
> _He'll have his assistant copy a few extra pages_.

13. make / the forms / her / Can / sign / you
_____?

14. delivered / You can / the package / tomorrow morning / have
_____.

15. before the party / the apartment / cleaned / having / They're
_____.

16. to call / the restaurant / She'll / someone / for a reservation / get
_____.

17. a sign / will have / The store manager / printed / to announce the sale
_____.

Match each step for planning a social event with the correct definition. Write the letter. You will not use all of the definitions.

> **Example:** arrange catering __h__

18. pick a date and time _____
19. make a list of attendees _____
20. set up the room _____
21. make a budget _____
22. assign responsibilities _____

a. tell people what to do
b. have invitations printed
c. get someone to play music
d. invite people to the party
e. change the appearance of the room
f. decide who to invite
g. decide how to spend the money
h. arrange for someone to make the food
i. choose when to have the party

UNIT 3 — Achievement Test (continued) Name _____

Look at the pictures. Use the passive causative to write a sentence about the service that each person wants.

Example:

Stan _wants to have a package delivered_.

23. Annie _____.

24. Harry _____.

25. Irene _____.

UNIT 3 — Achievement Test (continued) Name _____

Read the article. Then read it again and match each sentence beginning with the correct ending. Write the letter. You will not use all of the sentence endings.

Book of the Month

Home and Family magazine talked to Pamela Darby, author of the new book *Time Management*. Here's some of the advice that she gives:

Making time for special treatments and things you enjoy is important. You make time for a lot of things that you *don't* enjoy, like work and housecleaning. Choose something that you really like to have done, make an appointment, and go. You could get your nails done or have someone massage your back. The important thing is to choose something that you enjoy having done.

Accept offers of help. People are so used to doing things on their own, that they don't think about letting people help them. If someone asks, "How can I help?" tell them what you need done! For example, if you're planning a class party for one of your children, get some of the other parents to bring food. When someone offers to watch the kids, let them do it!

But, you don't have to wait for people to offer to help. Assign responsibilities to other family members. Have your spouse drop off the dry cleaning on the way to work. Get your kids to help around the house. Even young children can be responsible for certain tasks, such as putting away their toys or setting the table.

If you like these ideas, then read Pamela Darby's new book, *Time Management*, and learn how to use your time better.

Example: Make time ___g___

26. Have something _____
27. Have other people _____
28. Tell people _____
29. Get your family to _____
30. Get this book _____

a. help with things you need to do.
b. planned, like a big party.
c. to help you manage your time.
d. do tasks around the house.
e. how to do things your way.
f. when you need help.
g. for things that you enjoy.
h. do all of your work, including housecleaning.
i. done, like a massage treatment.

4

UNIT 3 — Achievement Test (continued) Name

Choose one of the following topics to write about. Write four or five sentences.

- Imagine that you are planning a party with some friends or family. Who is the party for and why? Who will you get to help you plan the event? What things will you have them do?

- Your neighbor has just moved to town and has asked you to recommend services you use regularly. Think of the one you use most. What kind of business is it? What can you get done there? Describe the quality and workmanship.

31–33. _____

UNIT 4 Achievement Test

Name _____

Track 05

🔊 **Listen to the conversations. Read the types of books listed in the box. Then listen again and write the type of book each person is talking about.**

| ~~mystery~~ | thriller | romance novel | science fiction |
| biography | autobiography | travel book | short stories |

Example: _____mystery_____

1. _____
2. _____
3. _____
4. _____
5. _____
6. _____
7. _____

Complete each sentence. Circle the letter of the correct answer.

Example: I love games and trying to figure things out, so I really like to _____.
  (a.) do puzzles   **b.** read aloud   **c.** curl up

8. My husband and I are trying to decide how to decorate our living room. So I buy decorating magazines and _____ to give us some ideas.
   a. curl up   **b.** read articles online   **c.** do puzzles

9. My grandfather can't see very well anymore, but he loves books. So sometimes I _____.
   a. listen to audio books   **b.** do puzzles with him   **c.** read aloud to him

10. This _____ keeps you guessing the entire time. You can't wait to find out what's going to happen next.
    a. trash   **b.** cliff-hanger   **c.** memoir

11. I don't have time to read every word of my magazines. I _____ quickly to see which articles interest me the most.
    a. read e-books   **b.** skim through them   **c.** listen to them

12. This book is a _____ that's perfect for a vacation—it's not very challenging, but enjoyable.
    a. best-seller   **b.** cliff-hanger   **c.** fast read

1

UNIT 4 — Achievement Test (continued) Name _____

Check the correct sentences.

Example: ☐ We all think whether this comic is the best.
☑ We all think that this comic is the best.

13. ☐ I was surprised that he wrote another book.
    ☐ I was surprised why he wrote another book.

14. ☐ Do you know where did Tina leave the magazine?
    ☐ Do you know where Tina left the magazine?

15. ☐ I wonder if she liked the movie.
    ☐ I wonder did she like the movie.

16. ☐ Did he like the food? I guess not.
    ☐ Did he like the food? I don't guess so.

17. ☐ I'd like to know whose jacket is this.
    ☐ I'd like to know whose jacket this is.

18. ☐ Tell me what is the novel about.
    ☐ Tell me what the novel's about.

19. ☐ I don't know if we'll be late, but I hope not.
    ☐ I don't know if we'll be late, but I don't hope so.

Use each question to complete the embedded question.

Example: Did Carla borrow my magazine?
I can't remember ___if Carla borrowed my magazine___.

20. Did The Book Barn have a sale on paperbacks last week?
    Could you tell me _____?

21. Do they sell newspapers at the little store down the street?
    I wonder _____.

22. Where did you find the article about low-calorie desserts?
    I'd like to know _____.

23. Why do more people read comics in Japan than in Brazil?
    I'm curious _____.

UNIT 4 — Achievement Test (continued) Name _____

Read the book reviews. Then read them again and check true or false.

Book Review

Are you looking for something good to read? Read our reviews of some bestsellers and award-winning books.

Guinness Book of World Records
by various authors

First published in Great Britain in 1955, a new edition is made every year. This book contains information about world records of all kinds. Some of the most popular categories include world records in sports, nature, movies, TV, music, and human achievements. With color photographs and lots of fun facts, this book is popular with adults and children.

One Hundred Years of Solitude
by Gabriel García Márquez (Colombia)

This novel tells the story of the town of Macondo. It starts with the founding of the town by a member of the Buendia family and ends over one hundred years later with its destruction by a severe hurricane. The story follows six generations of the Buendia family and witnesses their passions and emotions, strengths and weaknesses, and successes and failures.

Long Walk to Freedom
by Nelson Mandela (South Africa)

Winner of the Nobel Peace Prize and the first democratically elected president of South Africa, Nelson Mandela tells his life story in this moving book. He recalls his childhood, learning about black-white relations, and his belief that all people, black and white, must be free. He wrote much of the book secretly during the twenty-seven years he spent in prison. Mandela finishes his story with the day he became president—a day he said his "long walk to freedom" had just begun.

The Old Man and the Sea
by Ernest Hemingway (U.S.)

This simple but powerful novel is about Santiago, an old Cuban fisherman who hasn't caught a fish in eighty-four days. He goes farther out into the water and finally hooks a huge fish. But the fish is very strong and pulls the boat. For two days Santiago fights and tries to control the fish. He admires its strength and courage, but won't let it go. It's a classic story of a hero who will not be defeated.

		true	false
Example:	The *Guinness Book of World Records* is a collection of short stories.	☐	☑
24.	The *Guinness Book of World Records* contains information about travel in Great Britain.	☐	☐
25.	*One Hundred Years of Solitude* is a memoir about the survivors of a hurricane.	☐	☐
26.	*Long Walk to Freedom* is a novel about growing up in South America.	☐	☐
27.	*The Old Man and the Sea* is a fictional story about a hero.	☐	☐

UNIT 4 — Achievement Test (continued) Name _____

Complete each embedded question in your own way.

Example: After you read it, tell me ___whether this book is any good___.

28. I'd really like to know _____.
29. I'm curious _____.
30. I was wondering _____.

Choose one of the following topics to write about. Write four or five sentences.

- Think about different reading materials and/or different types of books you have read. Why do you like or dislike them? Discuss their value.
- Discuss your reading habits.

31–33. _____
_____
_____
_____
_____
_____
_____
_____
_____
_____

UNIT 5 Achievement Test

Name _____

Track 06

🔊 **Listen to the news reports. Read the statements. Then listen again and check the answer that correctly completes each sentence.**

> **Example:** The problem is a _____.
> ☐ drought   ☑ typhoon   ☐ tornado

1. The reporter is describing a _____.
   ☐ flood   ☐ tornado   ☐ drought

2. The storm will probably be _____.
   ☐ catastrophic   ☐ moderate   ☐ mild

3. According to the report, the death toll is _____.
   ☐ high   ☐ not known   ☐ low

4. There _____ from the landslide.
   ☐ are no deaths   ☐ are no survivors   ☐ is no property damage

5. This report mentions supplies you should have _____.
   ☐ in case of an evacuation   ☐ in a shelter   ☐ in a first-aid kit

Match each picture with the correct sentence. Write the letter. You will not use all of the sentences.

Example: _d_

a. There was a flood yesterday.
b. There was a lot of destruction.
c. It hasn't rained in six months.
d. It was 8.2 on the Richter scale.
e. Luckily, there were very few injuries in the landslide.
f. There must be a power outage.
g. The hurricane has brought high winds and rain.

6. ____

7. ____   8. ____   9. ____

1

UNIT 5 — Achievement Test (continued) Name _____

Read each sentence and check true or false.

	true	false
Example: A hurricane is a natural disaster.	✔	☐
10. A severe earthquake is generally more dangerous than a mild one.	☐	☐
11. A tornado is the result of a long period of time with no rain.	☐	☐
12. An evacuation removes people from dangerous places.	☐	☐
13. A first-aid kit is a supply of non-perishable food items.	☐	☐

Change each statement from direct speech to indirect speech, changing the verb in the indirect speech statement. Change the pronoun if necessary.

Example: The police said, "Three people were injured during the typhoon."
The police said (that) three people had been injured during the typhoon.

14. Dad said, "The batteries in the flashlight need to be changed."
_____

15. The weather forecaster said, "It is the worst storm in fifty years."
_____

16. The mayor of the town said, "Evacuate immediately."
_____

17. The doctor told them, "It's important to get vaccinations before your trip."
_____

18. The TV reporter said, "Thousands of people were affected by the flood."
_____

19. The emergency workers said, "Don't leave your homes yet."
_____

Complete each sentence with say or tell.

Example: Didn't anyone ___tell___ you the news?

20. What did the police _____ about the emergency?

21. The experts _____ this is going to be the worst storm of the season.

22. Can you _____ me what you heard during the weather report?

23. They _____ that everyone should leave before the storm.

2

UNIT 5 — Achievement Test (continued) Name _____

Read the web page. Then read it again and check yes, no, or no information.

@Pompeii

http://www.romehistory.com/pompeii

POMPEII

Death of a City

On the morning of August 24, 79 C.E., Pompeii was a wealthy Roman city full of people and life. No one thought that in two days the city would become a grave for 2,000 people.

Pompeii is located 8 km from Mt. Vesuvius. The mountain had once been an active volcano, but it had never erupted during the lifetime of anyone in the city. People were, however, used to earthquakes. Perhaps that is why when the earth shook for days before the volcano erupted, no one panicked. People must have thought they were safe, but they were wrong.

The first sign of danger was a strange cloud rising from Mt. Vesuvius. It was a cloud of dark smoke and ash. For about eight hours, the cloud grew and covered a huge area beyond the city. The cloud carried rocks and ash, which fell over Pompeii like rain.

People evacuated the city in terror. That night, however, the rain of rocks and ash stopped. Many people thought the danger was over and returned to their homes.

Around 7:30 the next morning, about 2,000 people were walking around the city, probably looking at the damage from the day before. Suddenly, Mt. Vesuvius exploded, sending a landslide of hot rocks, fire, and gases towards Pompeii. In less than two minutes, it killed everything in its path, and buried the city.

The city was perfectly preserved and remained buried for almost 2,000 years. Now people can learn a lot about how the Ancient Romans lived from studying Pompeii.

---

	yes	no	no information
Example: Did the eruption of Mt. Vesuvius cause any casualties?	☑	☐	☐
24. Did anyone expect Mt. Vesuvius to erupt?	☐	☐	☐
25. Did people leave Pompeii when rocks and ash started falling?	☐	☐	☐
26. Did the volcano kill people in Pompeii slowly?	☐	☐	☐
27. Was the buried city of Pompeii discovered by accident?	☐	☐	☐

UNIT 5 — Achievement Test (continued) Name _____

Complete each sentence in your own way. Use indirect speech.

Example: Yesterday a person told me _____that I looked nice_____.

28. When I was a child, people often said _____.

29. Last week someone told me _____.

30. Today someone said _____.

Choose one of the following topics to write about. Write four or five sentences.

- Describe one of the following natural disasters: flood, tornado, landslide, drought, or typhoon.
- What are some ways that people can prepare for an emergency?

31–33. _____

_____

_____

_____

_____

_____

_____

_____

_____

_____

UNITS 1-5 Review Test 1

Name _____

Track 07

🔊 Listen to the conversation. Read the sentences. Then listen again and check **true** or **false**.

	true	false
Example: The patient had an appointment a few days ago, but he canceled it.	☐	☑
1. The patient broke his tooth.	☐	☐
2. The patient called to make the appointment a few days ago.	☐	☐
3. The patient didn't call earlier because he was busy with work.	☐	☐
4. The dentist had already seen the patient's tooth before they had the conversation.	☐	☐

Track 07

🔊 Listen to the conversation. Read the sentences. Then listen again and circle the word or phrase that best completes each sentence.

Example: The man wants to (**send**/ receive / open) a package.

5. Maya thinks that Pack Express (**won't deliver / delivered / must be able to deliver**) the package to Lima overnight.

6. Maya told Steve that Pack Express (**was not efficient / was really good / won't be able to**).

7. When Steve used Aero Fast, they (**were extremely reliable / were not helpful / did a good job**).

Track 07

🔊 Listen to the radio announcement. Read the statements. Then listen again and check **true** or **false**.

	true	false
Example: The National Weather Service says to leave your house.	☐	☑
8. It's too dangerous for people to stay in their homes.	☐	☐
9. Right now, people in the area should prepare for an evacuation.	☐	☐
10. The radio announcer encourages people to read during the storm.	☐	☐
11. It's not necessary to have a flashlight ready.	☐	☐
12. There might be a power outage, so it is important to be prepared.	☐	☐

UNITS 1-5 — Review Test 1 (continued) Name _____

Look at the pictures. Check the sentence that matches each picture.

Example:
- ☐ I can't stop wheezing.
- ☑ I shouldn't eat so much.

13.
- ☐ Can you give me a ride? My hip hurts.
- ☐ Can you fill in for me? I have a pain in my chest.

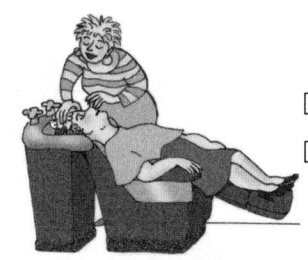

14.
- ☐ She's getting her hair washed.
- ☐ She might wash her hair.

15.
- ☐ They should have brought an umbrella.
- ☐ The storm might cause a flood.

16.
- ☐ He must not be able to drive.
- ☐ He may be stuck in traffic.

UNITS 1–5 • Review Test 1 (continued) Name _____

Circle the letter of the answer that correctly completes each sentence.

Example: Adam studied abroad in Russia, _____?
  a. didn't he   **b.** did Adam   **c.** doesn't he

17. By this time last year, the company _____ 2 million client orders.
  a. didn't fill   **b.** had filled   **c.** were filled

18. I'm speaking next, _____?
  a. am I   **b.** aren't I   **c.** I'm not

19. She asked me to call next week, so her news _____ very important.
  a. would not be   **b.** not be   **c.** must not be

20. I _____ see you tomorrow around noon. Why don't you come by then?
  a. can't   **b.** might   **c.** will be able to

21. The movie hadn't yet begun when _____.
  a. we arrive   **b.** we arrived   **c.** we had arrived

22. How do you get your children _____ fruits and vegetables?
  a. to eat   **b.** eats   **c.** might eat

23. Would you like to have the hotel room _____ while you're out?
  a. clean   **b.** cleaned   **c.** be able to clean

24. I asked my friend _____ me a ride to work.
  a. for giving   **b.** give   **c.** to give

25. We were disappointed _____ you couldn't come with us.
  a. that   **b.** if   **c.** where

26. The reporter said _____ for a severe storm.
  a. would prepare   **b.** to prepare   **c.** prepared

27. Jack didn't know _____ Mechanical Magazine.
  a. that I got   **b.** whether I didn't get   **c.** when did I get

28. They _____ that the disease can be deadly.
  a. say   **b.** tell   **c.** told

29. The radio announcer says _____ stay outside.
  a. don't   **b.** not to   **c.** didn't

UNITS 1–5 — Review Test 1 (continued) Name _____

Cross out the word in each group that doesn't match the category.

Example: medications: antibiotic   w~~heeze~~   nasal spray

30. ways to address someone: by first name   by their clothing   by title
31. types of medical treatments: conventional   homeopathy   appointment
32. emergency supplies: non-perishable foods first-aid kit   power outage
33. weather events: severe   landslide   drought
34. types of service: professional   reliable   mild
35. preparations for a meeting: assign responsibilities   get antacids   plan an agenda

Write an appropriate answer to each question. Use phrases from the box. You will not use all of the phrases.

I'll see what I can do.	It's in the autumn.	Please do.
At the newsstand around the corner.	~~Of course not!~~	Yes, a small gift is nice.
It's a novel.	Please call me Russell.	Yes, it really is.

Example: Do you mind if I ask you something?   _Of course not!_

36. It's too cold for a walk today, isn't it? _____
37. Can I have the copies made for this afternoon? _____
38. Should I bring something to a person's home when I'm invited for dinner? _____
39. What kind of book is it? _____
40. What do you like to be called? _____
41. Could you tell me where you bought that magazine? _____

UNITS 1–5 — Review Test 1 (continued) Name _____

Answer each question in your own way. Write complete sentences.

Example: What might you be able to do next year?
I might be able to visit you in Mexico.

42. What is something that you had done before you were 15 years old?
_____

43. What is something that you might get done for a social event?
_____

Read each situation. Write a complete sentence, following the instructions in parentheses.

Example: You are calling a doctor's office because you'd like to make an appointment today. (Use I wonder.)
I wonder if I might be able to see the doctor today.

44. You're talking to a friend. You think that he knows where you live, but you want to make sure. (Write a tag question.)
_____

45. You're talking to a friend. She broke a tooth last night, but she hasn't been able to see a dentist yet. (Use must to make a conclusion.)
_____

46. Yesterday someone told you some news. Report the news to a friend. (Use reported speech.)
_____

UNITS 1–5 ▬ **Review Test 1** (continued) **Name** _____

Read the newspaper column. Then read it again and check <u>yes</u> or <u>no</u> for each question.

Ask Globe Trotter

Dear Globe Trotter,

My roommate is from Vietnam, and she has invited me to her parents' home for a typical Vietnamese dinner. I'm excited, but nervous about not knowing the correct etiquette. Can you give me some tips?

Sincerely,
Hungry to Learn

Dear Hungry to Learn,

It's great that you want to be culturally literate! Here are some things to keep in mind at dinner:

- It's polite to take a small gift to your hosts, such as sweets, tea, or coffee. Flowers are an acceptable gift. But don't take white ones—white is the color of death.
- It's customary to take off your shoes before entering someone's home.
- People traditionally bow when they are introduced, but some people also shake hands. It's best to wait and see what the other person does.
- If you have trouble with chopsticks, mention your lack of skill and ask for a fork.
- Use two hands to pass a plate to someone or to accept one.
- If you are offered a second or third portion of food, you must accept it. (If you don't, it might be considered offensive.)
- Lastly, if you don't know what to do, it's OK to ask.

Sincerely,
Globe Trotter

		yes	no
Example:	Had "Hungry to Learn" been culturally literate about Vietnam before she wrote to Globe Trotter?	☐	☑
47.	Are yellow flowers an acceptable gift to take to dinner at a Vietnamese home?	☐	☐
48.	Is it taboo to ask for a fork?	☐	☐
49.	Is it OK to say "no" if a Vietnamese host offers you more food?	☐	☐
50.	Is it impolite to ask a Vietnamese host a question about table manners?	☐	☐

UNITS 1–5 — Review Test 1 (continued) Name _____

Read the newspaper column again and circle the letter of the correct answer.

Example:	"Hungry to Learn" _____ dinner with her friend's family.		
	a. doesn't want to have	b. has to have	(c.) wants to have

51. "Hungry to Learn" _____ Vietnam.
    a. doesn't know table etiquette from
    b. is culturally literate about
    c. lives in

52. In this column, "Globe Trotter" <u>doesn't</u> give advice about _____ in Vietnam.
    a. etiquette
    b. table manners
    c. time and punctuality

53. People _____ take off their shoes before they go inside a Vietnamese home.
    a. never
    b. usually
    c. rarely

54. A Vietnamese person _____ bow when they meet someone for the first time.
    a. might
    b. must
    c. may be able to

Choose two of the following topics to write about. Write at least six sentences about each.

- greetings and meeting someone for the first time
- good etiquette for males and females in your country
- medications you use for specific symptoms or medical problems
- a service you've been happy or unhappy with and why
- an emergency, severe weather event, or natural disaster
- reading and literature in your country

Topic: _____

55–57. _____

_____

_____

_____

_____

Topic: _____

58–60. _____

_____

_____

_____

_____

UNITS 1-5 Speaking Test 1

Name _____

UNITS 1-5 — Speaking Test 1 (continued) Name _____

Picture response questions

1. [Point to the man exiting the dentist's office into the waiting room.] Look at the patient leaving the dentist's office. Make a conclusion about the service at this office with <u>must</u>.

2. [Point to the receptionist on the phone with the man.] A patient has called to make an appointment. Create a conversation for the receptionist and this patient.

3. [Point to the two women talking.] These women are making small talk. Create a conversation for them.

4. [Point to the male patient holding his mouth in pain.] What's wrong with the man?

5. Look at the picture. Say as much as you can. [Encourage students to say more.]

Personal questions

6. What is something you had already done by the year 2009?

7. What is a natural disaster that can happen in this country? What should people do if this occurs?

8. What are some services you usually have done for you? Why do you use these services? What are some businesses that offer these services? What quality of service do you get from them?

9. Recommend a book, type of book, or other reading material that you enjoy. Why do you recommend it?

10. How would our lives be different if we didn't have books or libraries?

UNIT 6 Achievement Test

Name _____

Track 08

🔊 **Listen to the conversation. Read the questions. Then listen again and check yes or no.**

	yes	no
Example: Did Alan get lost?	☐	☑
1. Did Alan leave the office at 5:30?	☐	☐
2. Did Alan answer the phone?	☐	☐
3. Did they make a reservation at the restaurant?	☐	☐

Track 08

🔊 **Listen to the conversation. Look at the chart. Then listen again and check the reason Christina changed her mind about each activity.**

	Her tastes changed.	It's hard to make a living.	She didn't pass the exam.	Her parents talked her out of it.	She changed her mind.
Example: study art		✓			
4. study at a beauty school					
5. work at an art gallery					
6. play in a band					
7. work at a bank					

Complete the conversation. Use was going to or were going to.

Sally: Beth Goodman? Hi! Long time no see.

Beth: Wow, Sally Sanders! What are you doing these days?

Sally: Well, actually, now I'm Sally Finch. I got married last year.

Beth: But I thought you ___were going to___ marry Tommy Harrigan!
                                   Example

Sally: I _____ marry him, but I changed my mind and I didn't.
                    8.
What about you? I remember you _____ move to another city.
                                                        9.

Beth: Well, my sister and I _____ go to Toronto after high school.
                                              10.

Sally: Now I remember! Your sister was a great dancer, and she _____
                                                                                            11.
study ballet.

Beth: She was, but my parents talked her out of it.

1

UNIT 6 — Achievement Test (continued) Name _____

Match each sentence to one with a similar meaning. Write the letter. You will not use all of the sentences.

Example: I have a good memory. __c__

12. I have knowledge of the subject. _____
13. I have a lot of talents. _____
14. I have a lot of skills. _____
15. I have experience with the subject. _____

a. I'm very reliable.
b. I have learned a lot of abilities.
c. I remember things well.
d. I have worked with the subject before.
e. I was born with a lot of abilities.
f. I'm familiar with and understand the subject.

Circle the letter of the answer that correctly completes each sentence.

Example: If Diane isn't at the meeting, then she _____ an accident. It's the only reason she wouldn't be here.
   a. couldn't have had   b. may have had   (c.) must have had

16. I used to daydream a lot when I was younger, and now I regret it. I _____ so much time daydreaming.
   a. must have spent   b. shouldn't have spent   c. could have spent

17. We don't know what time Mike left. He _____ at 8:30, or it's possible that he left at 9:00.
   a. may have left   b. must have left   c. would have left

18. Brian had two choices after college. He _____ a job with IMB, but he decided to work for Orden instead.
   a. could have taken   b. shouldn't have taken   c. must have taken

19. Kim had to stop by the office this morning. She _____ something yesterday.
   a. must have forgotten   b. would have forgotten   c. should have forgotten

20. Felicia stopped painting at an early age. She _____ a huge success, but now we'll never know.
   a. couldn't have been   b. should have been   c. might have been

21. She really wanted that job. She _____ disappointed when she didn't get it.
   a. could have been   b. would have been   c. must have been

UNIT 6 — Achievement Test (continued) Name _____

Read the article. Then read it again and match the correct response to each question. Write the letter. You will not use all of the responses.

✓ TIPS FOR
Improving Your Interview

Congratulations! You have a job interview. Here's how to do your best:

○ **Prepare** Before the interview, read the job description and think about how your skills, abilities, and experience match the requirements of the position. Decide how you'll explain that information.

○ **Dress the part** Although employees of many companies wear casual clothes to work, you should dress formally for an interview. Always wear a suit to look professional.

○ **Arrive on time** Make sure to arrive on time or a few minutes early. Most interviewers agree: There's no excuse for being late.

○ **Don't be too friendly** An interview is a professional meeting. You should be energetic and enthusiastic, but not informal.

○ **Use good communication skills** Listen to questions carefully. Before you give your answer, make sure that it's a correct response to the question.

○ **Ask questions** It's important to ask questions in an interview. It shows your interest in the position and in the company. Listen to what is said during the interview and ask for additional information later.

○ **Maintain the three C's** It's OK to feel nervous—inside. But on the outside, you need to stay **C**ool, **C**alm, and **C**onfident. Remember, you can do the job; make sure the interviewer knows it, too.

Example: Why should you read the job description before the interview? __c__

22. Why should you always be on time for an interview? _____

23. Why shouldn't you be too friendly in an interview? _____

24. Why should you ask questions in an interview? _____

a. There's no excuse for being late.

b. You should be cool, calm, and confident.

c. You need to think about how you'll tell the interviewer about your skills.

d. It shows that you are interested in the job.

e. It is a formal occasion.

UNIT 6 — Achievement Test (continued) Name _____

Read the article again. Then circle the letter of the answer that best completes each sentence.

Example: You _____ be on time or a little early for an interview.
    (a.) have to   **b.** can   **c.** might

25. You _____ wear formal clothes to an interview.
    a. should   **b.** shouldn't   **c.** can never

26. You _____ think before you answer a question in an interview.
    a. should never   **b.** must   **c.** would

27. You need to show the interviewer that you _____.
    a. can do the job   **b.** are nervous   **c.** already have a job

Answer each question in your own way. Write complete sentences.

Example: You're waiting for a friend, but he is late. What do you think might have happened to him? _____He might have gotten lost._____

28. What is one thing that you should have done differently in your life?
_____

29. What is one skill, talent, or ability that you have?
_____

30. When you were a child, what did you think you would be when you grew up?
_____

Choose one of the following topics to write about. Write four or five sentences.

- Think about a job you want (or a job you have). Why do you think you would be good at that job? Write about your skills, abilities, experience, or knowledge.
- Think about a work or life decision that you regret. Express regret, possibility about the past, and a conclusion about the result of this decision.

31–33. _____
_____
_____
_____
_____
_____

UNIT 7 Achievement Test

Name _____

🔊 **Listen to the conversations. Look at the pictures. Then listen again and write the letter of the picture that matches each conversation.**

Example: __e__

1. _____
2. _____
3. _____
4. _____
5. _____
6. _____
7. _____

a.

b.

c.

d.

e.

f.

g.

h.

Match each word with the correct definition. You will not use all of the definitions.

Example: remember the dead __e__

8. picnic _____
9. newlyweds _____
10. wedding _____
11. engagement _____
12. honeymoon _____

a. a large bunch of flowers
b. agreement to marry someone
c. vacation taken by people after their wedding
d. marriage ceremony
e. think about people who have died
f. a meal eaten outside
g. people who were recently married

1

UNIT 7 — Achievement Test (continued)   Name _____

Underline the adjective clause and circle the relative pronoun in each sentence. Then draw an arrow from each relative pronoun to the noun or pronoun that it describes.

> **Example:** A person (who) is invited to dinner can take flowers.

13. Rosh Hashana is a religious holiday that celebrates the Jewish new year.

14. Valentine's Day is a great holiday for people who are in love.

15. The fireworks that are on the 4th of July are fantastic!

16. On December 26, Boxing Day is celebrated by people who live in Canada.

17. Anyone who wears a costume can participate in the Halloween parade.

Read each sentence. Write C if the adjective clause is correct. Write I if the adjective clause is incorrect, and fix the error.

> **Examples:** On Memorial Day, people remember soldiers who have died in wars. __C__
>
> The women we saw ~~they~~ were wearing kimonos. __I__
>
> The band ^that^ played at the festival is popular all over Latin America. __I__

18. They are the couple who they were married on the beach yesterday. ____

19. People give each other gifts that are handmade. ____

20. Anyone wants to see the fireworks can go to the lake and watch them. ____

21. "Happy Birthday" is a song that is well-known all over the world. ____

22. The cancan is a traditional dance that it comes from France. ____

Read the article. Then read it again and circle the word or phrase that correctly completes each sentence.

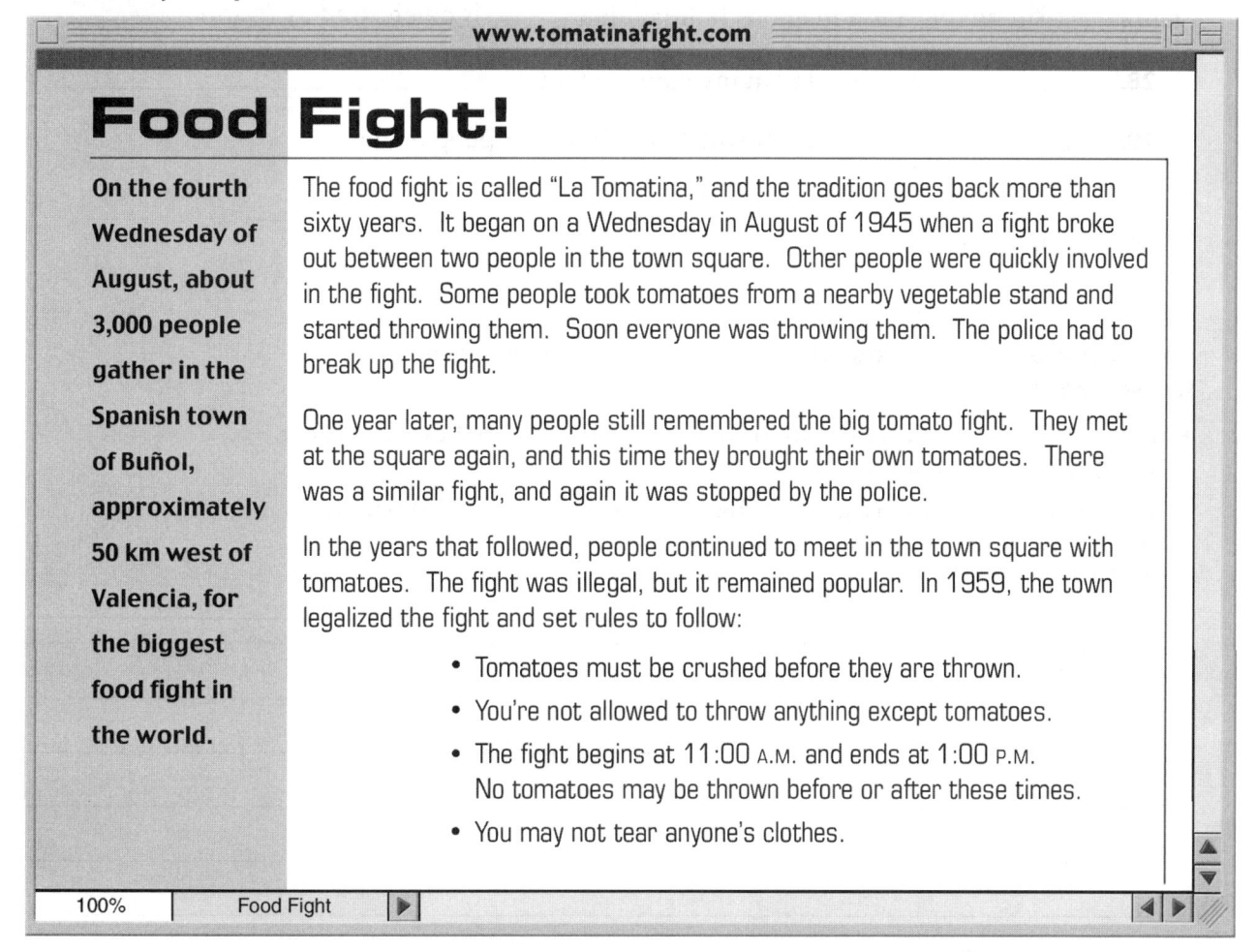

---

www.tomatinafight.com

Food Fight!

On the fourth Wednesday of August, about 3,000 people gather in the Spanish town of Buñol, approximately 50 km west of Valencia, for the biggest food fight in the world.

The food fight is called "La Tomatina," and the tradition goes back more than sixty years. It began on a Wednesday in August of 1945 when a fight broke out between two people in the town square. Other people were quickly involved in the fight. Some people took tomatoes from a nearby vegetable stand and started throwing them. Soon everyone was throwing them. The police had to break up the fight.

One year later, many people still remembered the big tomato fight. They met at the square again, and this time they brought their own tomatoes. There was a similar fight, and again it was stopped by the police.

In the years that followed, people continued to meet in the town square with tomatoes. The fight was illegal, but it remained popular. In 1959, the town legalized the fight and set rules to follow:

- Tomatoes must be crushed before they are thrown.
- You're not allowed to throw anything except tomatoes.
- The fight begins at 11:00 A.M. and ends at 1:00 P.M. No tomatoes may be thrown before or after these times.
- You may not tear anyone's clothes.

Example: La Tomatina is a (**historical** / seasonal / religious) holiday.

23. The fight is held in (**the town square** / **a vegetable market** / **Valencia**).

24. La Tomatina is a fight (**between two people** / **between the people and the police** / **involving a large group of people**).

25. Now La Tomatina is (**accepted** / **illegal** / **ignored**) by the police.

26. You (**should** / **have to** / **can't**) crush the tomatoes before you throw them.

27. (**Eating** / **Throwing** / **Making**) tomatoes is an important part of La Tomatina.

UNIT 7 — Achievement Test (continued) Name _____

Complete each sentence in your own way.

Example: ___Ramadan___ is a religious holiday that ___is celebrated by Muslims___.

28. _____ is a holiday in my country that _____.

29. _____ is/are a great way to celebrate for people who
_____.

30. I prefer holidays that _____.

Choose one of the following topics to write about. Write four or five sentences.

- Describe some wedding traditions in your country. What do people eat, wear, and/or do at a wedding?
- What is your favorite holiday? What type of holiday is it? What are some ways you commemorate this holiday? What are some traditions for this holiday?

31–33. _____
_____
_____
_____
_____
_____
_____

UNIT 8 Achievement Test

Name _____

Track 10

🔊 **Listen to the conversation. Read the statements. Then listen again and circle the word or phrase that correctly completes each sentence.**

> **Example:** Johnny (**accepts** /(**doesn't accept**)/ **would have accepted**) responsibility for what happened last year.

1. Johnny (**won / didn't win / didn't go to**) last year's competition.

2. Last year it (**didn't rain / must not have rained / rained**) at the competition.

3. If he wins the competition, Howard will (**start / keep / stop**) inventing things.

4. Howard thinks he (**can win / won't win / could have won**) the competition.

5. Brenda thinks that her invention is (**unique / low-tech / inexpensive**).

6. Brenda's invention helps people if they (**get lost / want something top-of-the-line / are inefficient**).

Complete each sentence with the correct form of the verb in parentheses.

> **Example:** If there ___is___ a commercial on TV, my husband always changes the channel.
> (be)

7. You _____ the announcement if you had stopped talking.
   (hear)

8. If more people _____ public transportation, there would be less air pollution.
   (take)

9. I'll call you tomorrow if we _____ to go to the movies.
   (decide)

10. We go to the park on weekends if it _____.
    (not rain)

1

UNIT 8 — Achievement Test (continued) Name _____

Cross out the word that is different from the others.

Example:	first-rate	innovative	leading	~~repetitive~~
11.	unique	usual	normal	customary
12.	high-tech	state-of-the-art	inefficient	cutting-edge
13.	top-of-the-line	first-rate	high-end	low-tech
14.	old-fashioned	revolutionary	novel	new

Read the advertisements and complete each sentence. Use words from the box. You will not use all of the words.

| efficient | ~~low-tech~~ | top-of-the-line |
| inefficient | state-of-the-art | wacky |

Example:
Finally—a cleaning machine that you can really use! It's not complicated. In fact, it's very simple. Nothing electrical, nothing cutting-edge! The most basic model available, it's ___low-tech___.

15.
Do you waste too much time cleaning? Try new Easy-Clean. This product will clean absolutely everything in your home quickly and easily.

It's very _____.

16.
If you're looking for the very newest technology in electronic products, then come to Electro-Tech. We have all the newest stereos, video games, televisions, computers, and much more! Everything in the store is _____.

17.
Are you tired of wearing the same boring clothes that everyone else wears? If you want things that are interesting, a little crazy, maybe even strange, then we have clothes for you! Visit Claudia's Closet on First Avenue.

Our clothes are _____.

18.
Do you want the very best shoes that money can buy? Golden Toe shoes aren't the cheapest shoes you can find, but they're the best. Try on a pair today. You'll see the difference of high quality. Our shoes are _____.

UNIT 8 — Achievement Test (continued) Name _____

Read the article. Then read it again and check <u>true</u> or <u>false</u>.

The Most Important Invention

Which of the following inventions do you think people would say is the most important: *the car, the toothbrush, the microwave, the computer, or the cell phone?*

If you answered *toothbrush*, then you agreed with 42% of the people who were asked this same question in a survey done by Massachusetts Institute of Technology.

Apparently, people have wanted clean teeth for a long time. From as far back as 3000 B.C.E., there is evidence of people chewing pieces of wood to clean their mouths. In Roman times, people began to clean their teeth by rubbing them with a piece of cloth. But neither of these methods was particularly effective.

So who deserves the credit for the low-tech, but efficient invention of the toothbrush? A Chinese emperor made the first toothbrush in 1498. It consisted of hard animal hair stuck into a piece of bone.

But toothbrushes didn't become popular immediately. They weren't commonly known until the 1600s. Even then, they were so expensive that all the family members in a house usually shared one!

Toothbrushes have come a long way since then. Nowadays, there are many versions for sale from basic, practical ones to state-of-the-art electric ones.

Even if you don't think the toothbrush is the most important invention, you probably agree that the world is a better, cleaner place because of it!

		true	false
Example:	Everyone agrees that the toothbrush is more important than other inventions.	☐	☑
19.	People didn't try to clean their teeth before toothbrushes were invented.	☐	☐
20.	Toothbrushes were made in Roman times, but they became popular in the 1600s.	☐	☐
21.	After toothbrushes became popular, it was common for people to share them.	☐	☐

UNIT 8 — Achievement Test (continued) Name _____

Read the article again. Then check the phrase that correctly completes each sentence.

> **Example:** If toothbrushes had been invented earlier, people probably _____.
> ☑ would have used them   ☐ wouldn't have liked them

22. If toothbrushes had been cheaper in the 1600s, people probably _____.
    ☐ wouldn't have used them   ☐ would have had their own

23. You would think like most people if you thought _____.
    ☐ the toothbrush was the most important invention   ☐ the toothbrush was invented in 1498

24. If people didn't use toothbrushes, _____.
    ☐ the world would be a better place   ☐ they wouldn't have clean teeth

Circle the letter of the sentence that correctly completes each conversation.

> **Example:** A: I'm sorry about the confusion.
> B: That's all right. _____.
>   **(a.)** It can happen to anyone
>   **b.** It wouldn't happen to you
>   **c.** It's top-of-the-line

25. **A:** I'm sorry I'm late.
    B: That's OK. _____.
      a. You'd better not be late
      b. No harm done
      c. I'm never late

26. **A:** How can I keep bugs away from me on the camping trip?
    B: I recommend this bug spray. _____.
      a. I think I'll treat myself
      b. It's entirely inefficient
      c. If you use it, bugs won't go near you

27. **A:** I'm sorry we didn't talk on the phone last night.
    B: Actually, _____. So I turned off my cell phone.
      a. I had tons of calls
      b. if you had called, I would have answered
      c. that depends

4

UNIT 8 — Achievement Test (continued) Name _____

Complete each sentence in your own way.

Example: If I want something that I can't afford, I usually *save my money until I can buy it*.

28. I usually go running if _____.

29. If I have extra time this weekend, I _____.

30. If I could buy anything I wanted, I _____.

Choose one of the following topics to write about. Write four or five sentences.

- Think about an event in your life. How would your life have been different if it hadn't happened?
- Describe an invention that is important to you. Discuss the impact it has had on you. Use some of the words from the box.

cutting-edge	efficient	first-rate	high-end	high-tech
inefficient	innovative	low-tech	novel	revolutionary
state-of-the-art	top-of-the-line	unique	wacky	

31–33. _____

UNIT 9 Achievement Test

Name _____

Track 11
🔊 **Listen to the discussion between a professor and his students. Read the questions. Then listen again and check true or false.**

	true	false
Example: The twentieth century was a difficult period in Russia.	✔	☐
1. In the beginning of the twentieth century, Russia was a monarchy.	☐	☐
2. Censorship was a problem under the monarchy.	☐	☐
3. Lenin was a conservative.	☐	☐
4. Stalin helped to create a democracy.	☐	☐
5. In Russia today, people choose government leaders by voting.	☐	☐

Look at the words in the box. Write them in order, from the word that describes a person who is <u>least</u> likely to want change to a person who is <u>most</u> likely to want change.

conservative	liberal	moderate	radical	~~reactionary~~

Example: ___reactionary___   strongly opposed to political or social change

6. _____

7. _____

8. _____

9. _____   strongly supporting political or social change

Complete the paragraph. Circle the word or phrase that correctly completes each sentence.

Example: Our country needs a new leader who will do a lot of (**the work / progress / (work)**) to make changes. Too many people are suffering from (**10**) (**poverty / justice / constitution**). We need new programs for (**11**) (**the education / education / school**). And (**12**) (**monarchy / health / dictatorship**) is another issue that must be addressed. What is my (**13**) (**help / advice / informations**) to voters? Support and vote for James Baldwin, because a vote for Baldwin is a vote for (**14**) (**progress / politics / news**).

1

UNIT 9 — Achievement Test (continued) Name _____

Check the sentence in each pair that is correct.

Example: ☑ The country can't afford to take action right now.
☐ The country can't afford citizens to take action right now.

15. ☐ The new program encourages young people to participate in government.
☐ The new program encourages to participate in government.

16. ☐ Many groups urge to vote.
☐ Many groups urge people to vote.

17. ☐ The dictator doesn't allow to speak against him.
☐ The dictator doesn't allow anyone to speak against him.

18. ☐ The king appears to be in control of the government.
☐ The king appears him to be in control of the government.

19. ☐ Several organizations offered to help after the disaster.
☐ Several organizations offered the victims to help after the disaster.

Circle the letter of the sentence that matches each picture.

Example:

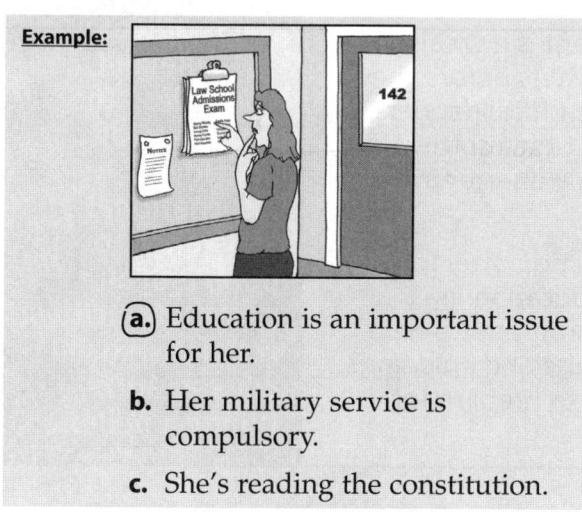

(a.) Education is an important issue for her.
b. Her military service is compulsory.
c. She's reading the constitution.

20. 
a. The woman voted for smoking indoors.
b. The woman is against smoking indoors.
c. The woman permits people to smoke indoors.

21. 
a. They don't believe in censorship.
b. People aren't permitted to read certain things.
c. People can write anything that they want.

22. 
a. They couldn't agree more.
b. They have a solution to the problem.
c. They are debating the issue.

UNIT 9 — Achievement Test (continued) Name _____

Read the web page. Then read it again and circle the word or phrase that correctly completes each sentence.

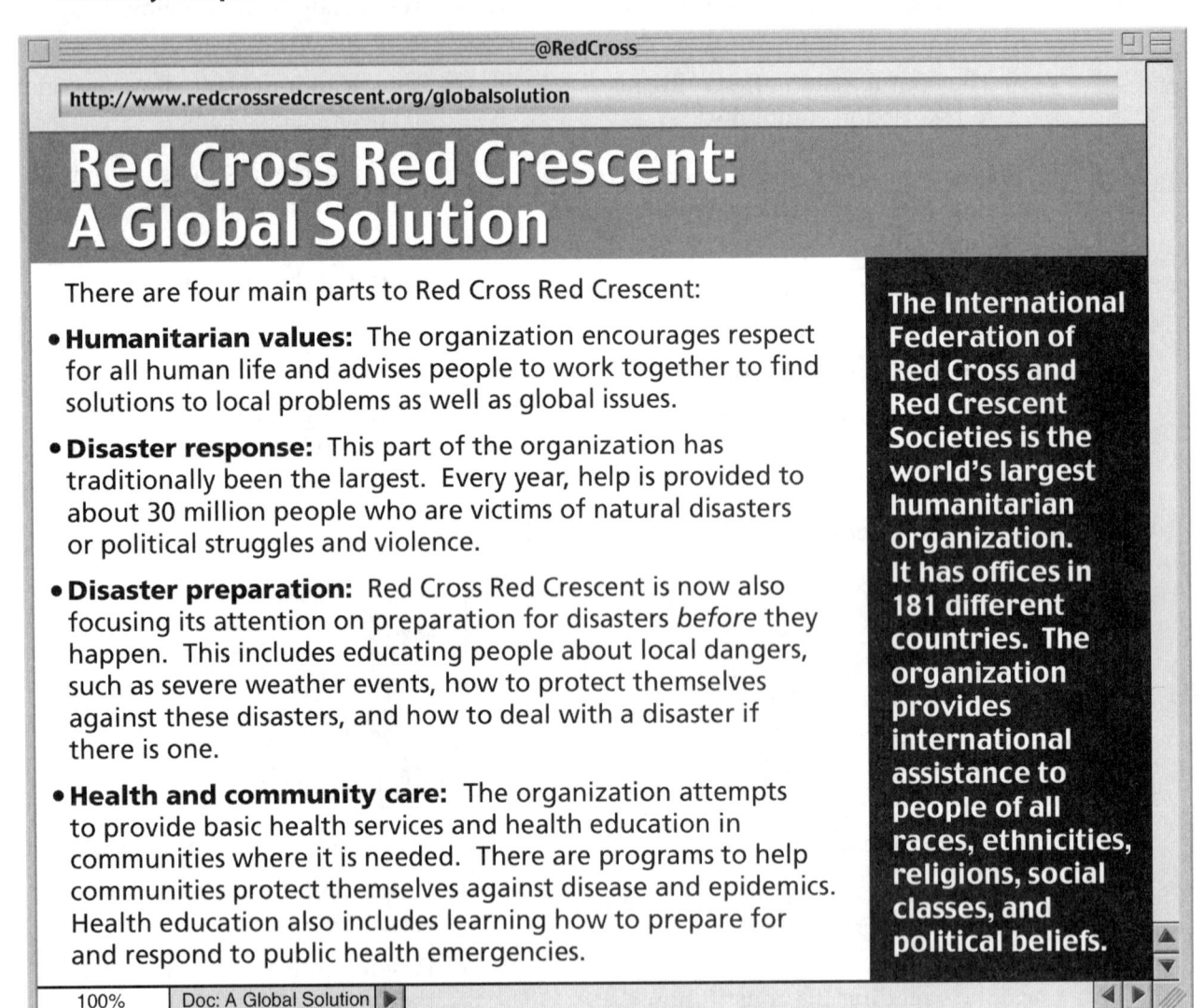

Red Cross Red Crescent: A Global Solution

http://www.redcrossredcrescent.org/globalsolution

There are four main parts to Red Cross Red Crescent:

- **Humanitarian values:** The organization encourages respect for all human life and advises people to work together to find solutions to local problems as well as global issues.

- **Disaster response:** This part of the organization has traditionally been the largest. Every year, help is provided to about 30 million people who are victims of natural disasters or political struggles and violence.

- **Disaster preparation:** Red Cross Red Crescent is now also focusing its attention on preparation for disasters *before* they happen. This includes educating people about local dangers, such as severe weather events, how to protect themselves against these disasters, and how to deal with a disaster if there is one.

- **Health and community care:** The organization attempts to provide basic health services and health education in communities where it is needed. There are programs to help communities protect themselves against disease and epidemics. Health education also includes learning how to prepare for and respond to public health emergencies.

The International Federation of Red Cross and Red Crescent Societies is the world's largest humanitarian organization. It has offices in 181 different countries. The organization provides international assistance to people of all races, ethnicities, religions, social classes, and political beliefs.

Example: Red Cross Red Crescent is a (**humanitarian** / political) organization.

23. The organization encourages people to (**do military service** / **work together**).

24. Red Cross Red Crescent works on solutions to (**peace** / **local and global issues**).

25. Every year 30 million people (**help** / **are**) victims of natural disasters.

26. The organization works with people before and after (**disasters** / **progress**).

27. With this organization, people (**can learn** / **can't afford**) to prepare for emergencies.

3

UNIT 9 — Achievement Test (continued) Name _____

Complete each sentence in your own way. You may use the issues from the box or other issues.

dictatorships	compulsory military service
democracy	capital punishment
lowering / raising the driving age	elections
peace	lowering / raising the voting age
racism	terrorism
war	censorship of news

Example: I'm against _____terrorism_____ no matter what because _I don't believe that it's OK to hurt another person for any reason_.

28. I'm in favor of _____ because _____.

29. I believe _____ is/are morally wrong because _____.

30. I think _____ is/are OK under some circumstances because _____.

Choose one of the following topics to write about. Write four or five sentences.

- Think of a problem in the world today. What are some possible solutions to this problem?
- What are some of your political and social beliefs? Discuss your position on an issue. Include both the pros and cons of the issue.

31–33. _____

UNIT 10 Achievement Test

Name _____

Track 12

🔊 **Listen to the conversation. Read the names of the places. Then listen again and match each place with Julie's description. Write the letter. You will not use all of the descriptions.**

Example: Miso-ha __b__

1. Agua Azul _____
2. Palenque _____
3. Sumidero Canyon _____

a. has spectacular scenery
b. is a must-see
c. is breathtaking
d. has a dangerous undertow
e. is in the jungle

Track 12

🔊 **Listen to the conversation again. Then circle the word or phrase that correctly completes each sentence.**

Example: Miso-ha is (**a waterfall**/ rocky / a valley).

4. There is a waterfall and a (**cave / cliff / canyon**) at Miso-ha.
5. The path to the waterfall can be (**slippery / exhausting / foggy**).
6. Palenque is (**a rainforest / in an arid valley / often foggy**) in the mornings.
7. Sumidero Canyon (**has lush plant life / is good for swimming / has caves**).

Write the letter of the picture that answers each question.

a.   b.   c.

d.   e.   f.

Example: Which picture shows arid scenery? __d__

8. Which picture shows a forest? _____
9. Which picture shows a steep hill? _____
10. Which picture shows a rocky path? _____
11. Which picture shows a cave? _____
12. Which picture shows flat land? _____

1

UNIT 10 — Achievement Test (continued) Name _____

Complete the paragraph with words from the box. You will not use all of the words.

breathtaking	pollution	environment	lush
canyon	power	environmentalists	undertow
cliffs	~~increase~~	Island	glacier

The government announced last week a plan to ____increase____ the development
(Example)

of hotels, homes, and commercial centers on Brilliant Beach, 12 km of land on the

southeastern coast of St. David's _____. There is now a debate between
                                       13.

the developers, who plan to begin building within six months, and _____,
                                                                        14.

who worry about the effects of development on the land, plants, and animals. The building

will start on the high _____ that look down on the beach and water
                              15.

below. The government has predicted that the _____ views of the water
                                                       16.

will bring tourists from all over the world. But environmentalists are concerned that with

development and tourists comes _____ and the destruction of the
                                         17.

environment.

Look at the map and complete the sentences with in, of, or on.

Example: The city of Colombo is ____on____ the island of Sri Lanka.

18. The city of Mumbai is _____ the west coast.
19. The Arabian Sea is west _____ India.
20. Chennai is _____ the southeast coast _____ India.
21. The island of Sri Lanka is southeast _____ India.
22. New Delhi is _____ the north.

2

UNIT 10 — Achievement Test (continued) Name _____

Read the web page. Then read it again and circle the letter of the answer that correctly completes each sentence.

ZIMBABWE

http://www.zimbabwe.gov/victoriafalls

VICTORIA FALLS

Victoria Falls in Zimbabwe is one of the most spectacular wonders of the natural world. The waterfall is almost 2 kilometers wide—one of the widest in the world.

Now world famous, the waterfall is Africa's number one tourist attraction. The area has been declared a national park and is protected from development.

There are a number of ways to view the breathtaking scenery of the area. Enjoy the calm water of the Zambezi River several kilometers north of Victoria Falls. Take a cruise on the river and watch local wildlife in its natural environment.

In contrast to the calm river north of the waterfall, the water south of it is fast, wild, and dangerous. For those who are very brave, this is one of the best places in the world for white-water rafting. But be careful, because it's too dangerous for people without experience to try.

There is a path through the rainforest near the falls for tourists. This lush jungle is home to a large variety of plants. Occasionally the path curves out of the rainforest to offer extraordinary views of the falls.

If you're not afraid to fly, then a helicopter ride provides a fantastic view of everything: the calm river, the falls, and the wild water at the bottom of the falls.

Give yourself several days to experience the area. You won't want to miss a thing!

Example: Victoria Falls is a _____.

    a. canyon   (b.) waterfall   c. rainforest

23. Victoria Falls is now a national park, and there _____ in this area.

    a. is no wildlife   b. is no development   c. are no tourists

24. Victoria Falls is _____ the calm water of the Zambezi River.

    a. south of   b. on the northern part of   c. on the edges of

25. White-water rafting is _____ for people without experience.

    a. especially enjoyable   b. not recommended   c. only

26. You can _____ in the rainforest.

    a. swim   b. walk   c. live

27. A helicopter ride is not a good idea for visitors who _____.

    a. don't like flying   b. want a fantastic view   c. usually travel by airplane

3

UNIT 10 — Achievement Test (continued) Name _____

Answer each question in your own way. Use too + an infinitive and a for phrase.

> **Example:** Why can't we play outside at 11:00 at night?
> _It's too dark for you to play outside at 11:00._

28. Why don't people usually swim in the winter?
_____

29. Why can't you walk from Rio de Janeiro, Brazil to Santiago, Chile?
_____

30. Why won't your family get up to exercise at 4:00 A.M.?
_____

Choose one of the following topics to write about. Write four or five sentences.

- Imagine that you and a friend went mountain climbing today. Include details about the scenery, views, and possible risks during your adventure.
- Think about global warming. What are some things you can do in your community to help curb it?

31–33. _____
_____
_____
_____
_____
_____
_____
_____
_____
_____

UNITS 6–10 Review Test 2

Name _____

Track 13

🔊 **Listen to the conversations. Read the statements. Then listen again and circle the letter of the phrase that correctly completes each sentence.**

> **Example:** The _____ catches the bridal bouquet.
> **ⓐ** next bride
> **b.** bride
> **c.** groom

1. Megan thought she would be a doctor, but she _____.
   a. settled on it   b. picked her brain   c. changed her mind

2. The man _____ a new car.
   a. doesn't need   b. is going to buy   c. is thinking about getting

3. The people bought the computer _____ a great price.
   a. because it was   b. without considering   c. even though it wasn't

4. The woman is probably _____.
   a. a swimmer   b. an environmentalist   c. a dictator

Track 13

🔊 **Listen to the conversation. Read the incomplete sentences. Then listen again and complete each sentence with a word or phrase from the box. You will not use all of the words.**

changed her mind	didn't want to	go on a picnic	parade
costume	fireworks	march in parade	should have thought
customs	gifts	movie	thought she would

> **Example:** Sarah doesn't know about the ___customs___ for Independence Day.

5. Sarah is going to _____ on Independence Day.
6. At first, Sarah _____ take soda to the picnic.
7. Sarah _____ about what to take to the picnic.
8. There is a _____ on Independence Day.
9. Sarah is going to watch _____ on Independence Day.

1

UNITS 6–10 – Review Test 2 (continued) Name _____

Track 13

🔊 **Listen to the conversation. Read the statements. Then listen again and circle the word or phrase that correctly completes each sentence.**

> **Example:** This conversation is about (**politics**/ the constitution / military service).

10. The Yellow Party is (**liberal / conservative / reactionary**).

11. The Yellow Party wants to fight (**terrorism / poverty / racism**).

12. The man (**is in favor of / disagrees with / isn't sure about**) making changes in government spending.

13. The woman (**totally agrees / couldn't agree more / doesn't agree**) with the man.

Look at the pictures. Check the sentence that matches each picture.

Example:
☑ He could have been a great artist if he tried.
☐ It's hard to make a living this way.

14.
☐ She must have forgotten her umbrella.
☐ She shouldn't have taken a taxi.

15.
☐ The family is decorating the room.
☐ The family got together for the holiday.

16.
☐ Today they are celebrating their engagement.
☐ They just got married.

17.
☐ It's really foggy. He must have gotten lost.
☐ It's really dangerous. He should be careful.

2

UNITS 6-10 – Review Test 2 (continued) Name _____

Cross out the word in each group that doesn't match the category.

Example:	types of holidays:	~~festival~~	seasonal	historical
18.	people at a wedding:	groom	tailor	bride
19.	types of abilities:	mathematical	athletic	urgent
20.	types of government:	politics	dictatorship	monarchy
21.	controversial issues:	puzzles	prohibiting smoking indoors	censorship
22.	natural settings:	forest	valley	tornado

Look at the pictures. Then circle the word or phrase that correctly completes each sentence.

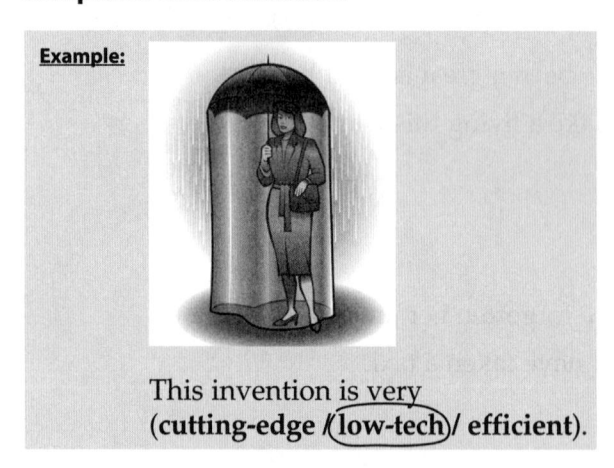

Example:

This invention is very (**cutting-edge** / **(low-tech)** / **efficient**).

23.

Be careful of those (**slippery** / **flat** / **exhausting**) steps.

24.

This government is (**a democracy** / **a dictatorship** / **a monarchy**).

25.

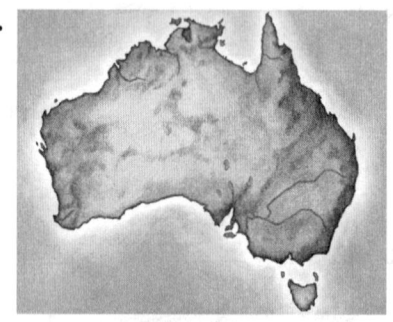

This map shows (**a canyon** / **a cave** / **an island**).

3

UNITS 6-10 — Review Test 2 (continued) Name _____

Circle the letter of the word or phrase that correctly completes each sentence.

> **Example:** Labor Day is a holiday _____ in September.
> a. that it takes place   (b.) that takes place   c. takes place

26. If you encourage everyone _____ one thing to the reception, then it won't be a lot of work.
a. to bring   b. bring   c. must bring

27. I _____ that movie, but I heard that it was awful, so I changed my mind.
a. must have seen   b. had already seen   c. was going to see

28. A birthday is a holiday _____ once a year.
a. that is celebrated   b. who celebrates   c. celebrates

29. Many people thought that the situation _____, but it didn't.
a. will improve   b. would improve   c. to improve

30. The person _____ the party should provide drinks and food.
a. who has   b. has   c. had already had

31. If he _____, he would have done better on the exam.
a. would have studied   b. studies   c. had studied

32. The conservatives wouldn't have won the election if they _____ the support of the reactionaries.
a. hadn't had   b. didn't have   c. wouldn't have had

33. _____ will be an important issue in the next election.
a. The healths   b. The health   c. Health

34. The airlines require _____ a passport for international travel.
a. all passengers to have   b. all passengers having   c. them having

35. We should _____ talking about controversial issues at the party last night.
a. avoided   b. avoid   c. have avoided

36. Because of the undertow, the sea is too dangerous _____.
a. for people to swim in   b. for people swimming   c. for swim

37. Senegal is _____ the west coast of Africa.
a. in   b. of   c. on

38. The mountain was _____, so we decided to end our hike that day.
a. too steep for us to climb   b. too steep to climb it   c. too steep to climbing

39. I convinced _____ letters to support raising the driving age to 21.
a. to write   b. my friends to write   c. my friends write

UNITS 6-10 — Review Test 2 (continued) Name _____

Read each group of sentences. Check the two sentences in each group that have a similar meaning.

> **Example:** ☑ Sandra is a conservative.
> ☐ Sandra wants the government to make changes.
> ☑ Sandra thinks that things are OK the way they are.

40. ☐ It's too spectacular to miss.
☐ You'd better not miss it.
☐ It's not worth seeing.

41. ☐ Would you say that's a touchy question?
☐ Are you a touchy person?
☐ Do you think that's too personal?

42. ☐ I just won't hear of it.
☐ I don't want to listen to you.
☐ I refuse to do it.

43. ☐ I couldn't agree more.
☐ I'm not sure I agree.
☐ I couldn't have said it better myself.

UNITS 6-10 — Review Test 2 (continued) Name _____

Read the web page. Then read it again and circle the letter of the answer that correctly completes each sentence.

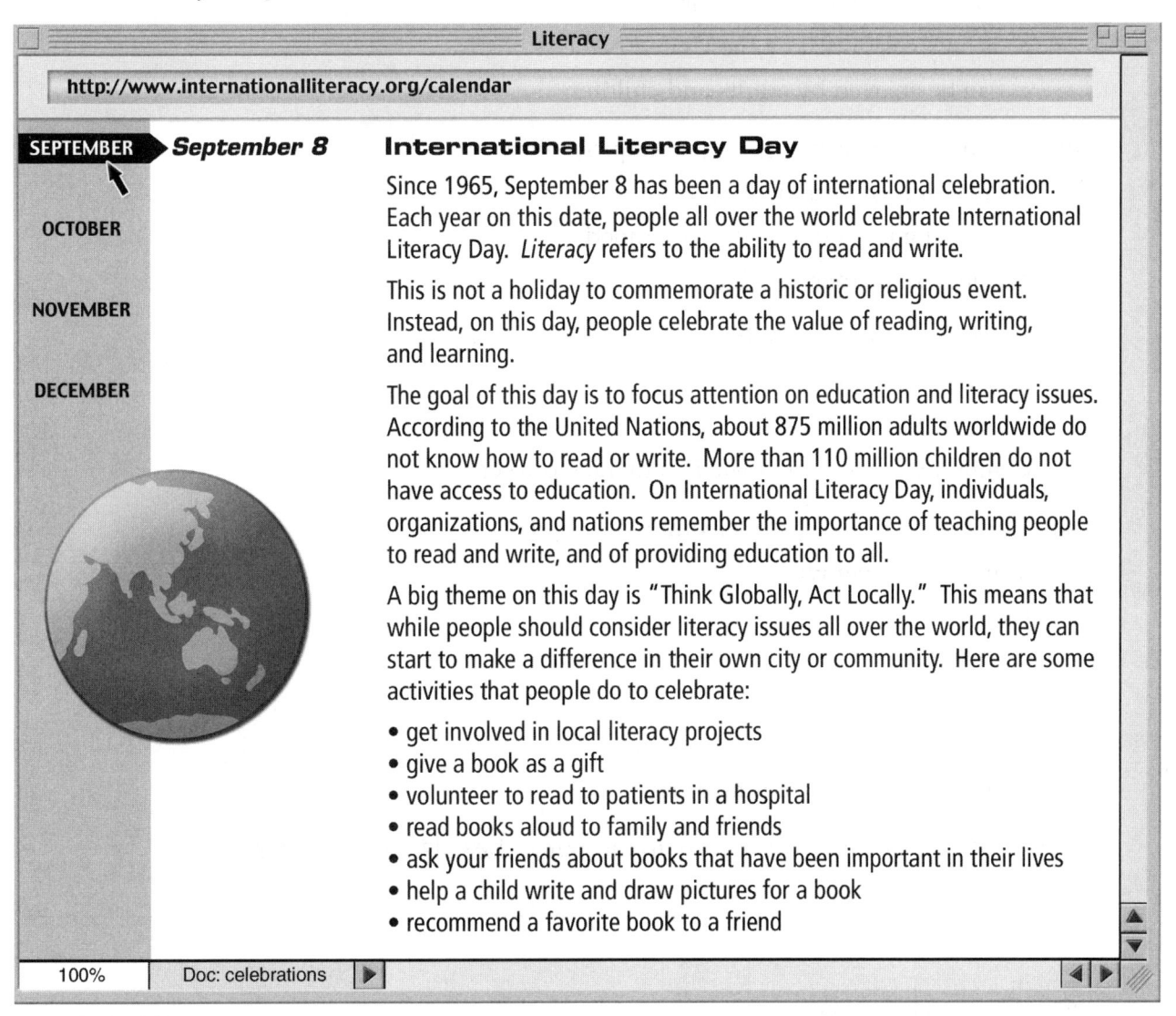

Literacy

http://www.internationalliteracy.org/calendar

SEPTEMBER

OCTOBER

NOVEMBER

DECEMBER

September 8 **International Literacy Day**

Since 1965, September 8 has been a day of international celebration. Each year on this date, people all over the world celebrate International Literacy Day. *Literacy* refers to the ability to read and write.

This is not a holiday to commemorate a historic or religious event. Instead, on this day, people celebrate the value of reading, writing, and learning.

The goal of this day is to focus attention on education and literacy issues. According to the United Nations, about 875 million adults worldwide do not know how to read or write. More than 110 million children do not have access to education. On International Literacy Day, individuals, organizations, and nations remember the importance of teaching people to read and write, and of providing education to all.

A big theme on this day is "Think Globally, Act Locally." This means that while people should consider literacy issues all over the world, they can start to make a difference in their own city or community. Here are some activities that people do to celebrate:

- get involved in local literacy projects
- give a book as a gift
- volunteer to read to patients in a hospital
- read books aloud to family and friends
- ask your friends about books that have been important in their lives
- help a child write and draw pictures for a book
- recommend a favorite book to a friend

Example: September 8 is a day to celebrate _____.
   a. reading, writing, and learning *(circled)*
   b. the end of censorship
   c. international holidays

44. The goal of this holiday is to _____.
   a. teach adults how to read
   b. get individuals to join reading programs
   c. think about education and literacy

UNITS 6-10 — Review Test 2 (continued) Name _____

45. International Literacy Day _____.

    a. started as a historical holiday

    b. is only celebrated by the United Nations

    c. can be enjoyed by adults and children

46. The article suggests _____ to improve literacy.

    a. traveling around the world

    b. working in your own neighborhood

    c. going to another country

47. If you want to celebrate International Literacy Day, you _____.

    a. should act globally

    b. have to buy a book

    c. might want to participate in a literacy project

48. People may _____ to celebrate this holiday.

    a. march in a parade

    b. pray

    c. give gifts

Complete each sentence in your own way.

Example: If I had gotten an extra ticket to the game, _I would have called you_.

49. I thought I would _____.

50. If I had more money, _____.

51. I didn't know _____.

52. If people didn't have cell phones, _____.

53. I think the government of this country should encourage people _____.

54. I should have _____.

UNITS 6–10 — Review Test 2 (continued) Name _____

Choose two of the following topics to write about. Write at least six sentences about each.

- a life decision that you've made
- a holiday that you celebrate
- an idea for a new invention
- your point of view on a controversial issue
- a natural setting in your country

Topic: _____

55–57. _____

_____

_____

_____

_____

_____

Topic: _____

58–60. _____

_____

_____

_____

_____

_____

UNITS 6-10 Speaking Test 2

Name _____

ST1

UNITS 6–10 — Speaking Test 2 (continued) Name _____

Picture response questions

1. [Point to the teenagers talking near the bookshelves.] What is he telling her? Complete the sentence for him.
2. [Point to the woman speaking to the librarian.] Why do you think she is looking for books about the Chinese New Year?
3. [Point to the two men talking to each other.] Create a conversation for these people.
4. [Point to the woman with the thought bubble (picture of valley and mountains).] What is she reading about? Describe the scenery. Say as much as you can.
5. Talk about the picture. Say as much as you can. [Encourage students to say more.]

Personal questions

6. What are some of your skills and talents?
7. Talk about changes in your life or work choices. What were you going to do? Why did you change your mind?
8. Talk about a holiday that you celebrate or a holiday that you have heard or learned about. How is it celebrated? What are some traditions associated with this holiday?
9. Are you more liberal, conservative, or moderate? Explain your feelings about one issue (such as censorship, prohibiting smoking indoors, or another issue).
10. Think about somewhere that is or could be dangerous. Describe the possible risks.

Audioscript

UNIT 1

Example: **A:** Good morning, I'm Vanessa Graham.
B: Hello, Mrs. Graham.
A: Actually it's *Ms.* Graham, please.

1. **A:** Excuse me. I'm looking for Dr. Guerra.
   B: I'll get him. But call him Manuel. Everyone uses first names here.
   A: OK, thanks.
   B: By the way, I'm Julia.
   A: Nice to meet you. I'm Neil.

2. **A:** Hello. I'm Ayako Suzuki. I'm here for the conference.
   B: I don't see your name here. Did you register?
   A: Yes, I did. In fact, I had already registered by the time the conference was announced.
   B: Oh, excuse me. Here it is.

3. **A:** Hey, Sophia. I'm making beef for dinner. Would you like to come over?
   B: Thanks, Mark, but I don't eat beef. There are rules against it in my culture.
   A: OK. Well maybe some other time. I can make chicken.
   B: Sounds good!

4. **A:** Hi, I'm Denise Pei.
   B: Hello, I'm Daniel Hoffman.
   A: Nice to meet you. By the way, how would you like to be addressed?
   B: Mr. Hoffman is fine, thanks.

5. **A:** What time are you going to dinner?
   B: The reservation is for 8:00, so I'll get to the restaurant after that.
   A: No! In this culture it's impolite to arrive late. You should be there no later than 8:00.

6. **A:** Why do your students call you *Ms.* Pilman instead of *Dr.* Pilman?
   B: Well, I had already taught them for a while when I became a doctor. They were used to calling me *Ms.* Anyway, titles really aren't important to me.

7. **A:** Hi, I'm Elizabeth Flores, the new English teacher.
   B: Hello, I'm Patricia Small. I'm a teacher here, too. I'll introduce you to everyone. How do you want the students to address you?
   A: What's customary here?
   B: Well, in our culture it's very impolite for a student to call a teacher by his or her first name.
   A: Then *Ms. Flores* is fine.

UNIT 2

Example: **A:** Nikki, what's wrong?
B: My head is killing me. I keep taking medicine, but it doesn't help.
A: You must feel terrible! You should go to the doctor.

1. **A:** Hello, I'm John Banks. I have a 2:00 appointment.
   B: OK. And what brings you in to the office today?
   A: One of my fillings came out.
   B: Oh no! How did you lose a filling?
   A: I don't know, but it really hurts!
   B: I'm sorry. The doctor will see you in just a minute.

2. **A:** Hi, Susan.
   B: Hi, Jim. You look awful.
   A: Thanks.
   B: No, I mean, you must feel terrible. Do you have a cold?
   A: No, I don't. It's my allergies. I forgot to take my allergy medication this morning. I can't stop sneezing. The trees and flowers are making my eyes red and itchy. I'm going to take something right now.

3. **A:** Is anything bothering you today, Mr. Kemper?
   B: No, Dr. Powell. I feel fine. I just came in to get my allergy shot.
   A: OK, I'll give you the shot, and you'll be out of here quickly.
   B: That's great. Thanks.

   ─────────────────────────

   A: Thanks for fitting me in this morning. I needed to see someone right away.
   B: Glad to be of help. What's the trouble?
   A: I think I broke a tooth.
   B: You must be in a lot of pain.
   A: Yeah, it's really killing me.
   B: Well, let's have a look. I might be able to fix it today.
   A: Will I need a prescription afterwards?
   B: Maybe. I might give you some painkillers.

UNIT 3

Julia: Hi, I'm your new neighbor. I just moved into apartment number 12. I'm Julia Frost.
Mark: I'm Mark Fines. Welcome to the neighborhood. Let me know if you need anything.
Julia: Actually, can you recommend a housecleaning service? I'd like to get the apartment cleaned before I unpack.
Mark: Sure. Almost everyone in the building uses Maid to Clean. They're very reliable.
Julia: Great. And what about a copy service? I have to get some things copied before Monday.
Mark: Go to Edison's. It's just down the street. They're really fast.
Julia: Edison's for copying. And can you tell me where you get your car repaired?
Mark: I always go to Tony's Auto Repair. They're not very efficient, but they're extremely helpful. They're around the corner.

Audioscript (continued)

Julia: And just one more question. Can you recommend a tailor?
Mark: Sure. Sew Good is great for tailoring. Their work is excellent, and they're very reasonable. They're across the street.
Julia: Thanks so much for your help. I appreciate it.
Mark: No problem. See you around!

UNIT 4

Example: **A:** Have you heard anything about this book?
B: Yeah, supposedly it's like all of his other books. You know, the police officer who desperately tries to solve a crime ...

1. **A:** What's this book about?
   B: There's this inventor, and he makes these robots that control people's minds. It's weird—it could never really happen.

2. **A:** Do you want any of these books?
   B: How about some nonfiction?
   A: Here's one about the life of Gandhi. In fact, he wrote it.

3. **A:** Can you recommend something very easy and light?
   B: Let's see ... oh, this is good! It's a love story about this couple whose parents won't let them get married.

4. **A:** I like to learn when I read.
   B: Well, this is a good book about the life of the Mexican painter Frida Kahlo. The author did a lot of research before writing. She used some of Frida's own letters to make it very personal.

5. **A:** Do you want this book?
   B: What is it?
   A: It's about Egypt ... how to get there, where to stay, what to see ...
   B: Well, I'm not planning a trip to Egypt, so I guess I'll pass.

6. **A:** Is this book scary?
   B: No, it's not scary, but it's very suspenseful and full of adventure. It's a real cliff-hanger. You can never guess what'll happen next.

7. **A:** Do you know anything about this book?
   B: Yes, it's fiction, but it's not a novel. It's a collection of works by different authors.

UNIT 5

Example: Our top story tonight is the typhoon that continues to take people's lives and destroy property. The storm is still very severe, and government officials are asking other countries for help.

1. The rain still hasn't stopped, and there's nowhere for the water to go. People's homes are becoming filled with water and many roads are covered as well. If you need to get somewhere, a boat will be more useful than a car.

2. Experts predict that the coming storm will be terrible. They feel certain that an evacuation will be necessary and that there will be a lot of destruction and many casualties. Some are even advising people to leave their homes now, before the storm hits.

3. Officials are trying to determine the number of people affected by yesterday's storm. However, it's difficult to determine casualties, because there is still a very large number of people who haven't been found. Search and rescue teams have been formed to look for survivors.

4. Although last week's landslide had a huge economic impact on the town of Hamilton, we are pleased to announce that the death toll from the disaster is zero.

5. You should always keep some supplies ready in case of minor injuries. Your supplies should include ointment, bandages, and painkillers.

REVIEW TEST 1 (UNITS 1–5)

A: Thanks for fitting me in.
B: Luckily, the dentist had a cancellation. What's bothering you today?
A: I lost a filling a few days ago, and now my tooth is killing me!
B: You lost it a few days ago? You should have called earlier!
A: I was going to, but I got busy with work.
B: Why don't you have a seat? The dentist will be right with you.

Steve: Hey, Maya, can you recommend a courier service? I need to send this package.
Maya: Sure, Steve. Why don't you have Pack Express take care of it?
Steve: Do you think that they can get it to Lima overnight?
Maya: They must be able to. They have service all over South America. They're really reliable.
Steve: I should have asked you for a recommendation earlier! Last week I used Aero Fast, but they were expensive and not very efficient.

Radio announcer: Tropical Storm Alex has arrived in our area. The National Weather Service says not to leave your house. It's too dangerous to drive, so if you're still in the area, you should stay inside and wait for the storm to pass. Curl up with a good book or do a puzzle. There's a possibility of a power outage, so be sure to have a flashlight or some candles nearby.

UNIT 6

A: I wonder where Alan is.
B: He must have gotten lost.
A: Oh, look, there he is. Hi, Alan!

AS2

Audioscript (continued)

C: Hi, guys. Sorry I'm late. I was going to leave the office at 5:30, but I got a call at 5:25. I shouldn't have answered the phone.
B: No problem. Now, let's talk about dinner! I thought we'd try the Indian place down the street.
A: Oh, we should have made a reservation for that place. It gets really busy.
B: Well, let's go look . . .

Simon: Hi, Christina. I'm Simon Wells, your career counselor. Let's look at your resume . . . So . . . you studied art, but you didn't graduate. What happened?
Christina: Well, it was going to be hard to make a living as an artist, so I quit.
Simon: And then you studied at a beauty school?
Christina: Yes, but I couldn't cut hair. I had this exam, but I didn't pass.
Simon: OK . . . and you have some job experience? You worked at an art gallery.
Christina: Yes, but I decided that I liked music better than art.
Simon: So your tastes changed?
Christina: Exactly! So I was going to play in a band, but my parents talked me out of it.
Simon: And then you worked at a bank?
Christina: Yes, I worked there for a few months, but then I didn't want to anymore. I guess I just changed my mind.
Simon: And now you want *my* help?
Christina: Yeah!

UNIT 7

Example: **A:** How can I give someone good wishes for the New Year?
B: Say, "Happy New Year!" The other person can answer, "Thanks, you too!" or "Happy New Year!"

1. **A:** My sister is getting married.
   B: Congratulations! What are weddings like here?
   A: The ceremony is simple. The real celebration is the reception. It's a big party with lots of food and dancing all night long.

2. **A:** Hey, Dan. Can I ask you something?
   B: Sure. What's up?
   A: I'm not sure of the customs here. I'm visiting someone's house tonight. Should I bring a gift for the host?
   B: Yes. You should take a small gift.
   A: Great. Thanks.

3. **A:** So, there's a holiday next week?
   B: Yes. Everyone travels to be with their relatives. The airports and train stations are mobbed. It takes a long time to get anywhere.

4. **A:** What are you doing?
   B: I'm sending some holiday cards.
   A: Is that a tradition here?
   B: Yes. Most people send cards to their friends and family.

5. **A:** How does your family celebrate Christmas?
   B: Well, we pray. Then we get together with friends and relatives and give each other gifts.
   A: That sounds nice.

6. **A:** I hear there's a holiday soon.
   B: That's right—Carnaval.
   A: How do you celebrate?
   B: Everyone wears a costume and goes out into the streets. It's so much fun!

7. **A:** I'm not sure of the customs here. I heard something about throwing flowers at a wedding?
   B: That's right—after the wedding ceremony, the bride throws her bouquet. All the single women try to catch it.

UNIT 8

Colleen: Hello, I'm Colleen Campbell for Channel 7 News. I'm reporting live from the Inventor's Cup in London. Inventors have gathered here from around the world to try to win first prize for the best invention. A few of the inventors are here with me now. Let's talk first to Johnny Nichols, who participated in last year's competition. What happened last year, Johnny?
Johnny: It wasn't my fault! It could've happened to anyone!
Colleen: Excuse me?
Johnny: I would have won if it hadn't rained and ruined my invention. I *still* can't believe it. Such bad luck . . . !
Colleen: OK, thanks, Johnny. Next is Howard Simon. Howard, the winner of today's competition gets a prize of 1,000 pounds. What will you do with the money if you win?
Howard: That's easy. I'll buy materials to invent more things.
Colleen: And if you don't win, will you try again next year?
Howard: Absolutely! If I compete every year, I'll win sooner or later.
Colleen: Well, good luck, Howard! Now let's go to Brenda Lipton. Brenda, your invention looks pretty high-tech.
Brenda: It is, and you won't find anything else like it. It's an entirely new idea.
Colleen: What does it do?
Brenda: It helps you if you get lost. See these colored buttons? If you touch the blue button, it tells you where you are.
Colleen: What happens if I touch the red button?
Brenda: Oh, I don't recommend that . . . Oops!
Colleen: I think that's it for this report. I'm Colleen Campbell reporting live. . . .

UNIT 9

Teacher: Good morning class! Let's open our books and discuss last night's reading on Russia. Throughout its history, Russia has been through many changes. Who can tell me more? Marcia?
Marcia: The most difficult period in Russia was probably the twentieth century. In 1917, Russia was a monarchy ruled by a czar, or king.

Audioscript (continued)

Teacher: What were some problems under the monarchy, Marcia?
Marcia: Problems such as poverty, poor health and education systems, and poor working conditions made the czar's politics unpopular.
Teacher: What did the people do? Jeff?
Jeff: The Russian people, under the leadership of Vladimir Lenin, formed a group called the socialist party. The members of the socialist party were radicals who wanted to change the way the country was ruled. Lenin and his supporters believed a revolution was necessary. The revolution was successful, and the monarchy lost its power. Russia invaded nearby countries and formed the Soviet Union.
Teacher: Right. What happened to the Soviet Union? Jessica?
Jessica: In 1922, Joseph Stalin became leader of the Soviet Union. He ruled the government with complete and total power. Under Stalin, the Russian people suffered greatly. If someone disagreed with him, he had that person arrested or even killed. Stalin's dictatorship continued until his death in 1953.
Teacher: Good. When were people able to vote in Russia?
Marcia: In 1990, under the leadership of Mikhail Gorbachev, people were able to vote in the Soviet Union. Elections were held and Gorbachev became the first president of the Soviet Union. Gorbachev, with others, wrote the first constitution in the history of the Soviet Union, which made it a democracy.

UNIT 10

Julie: Hey, Mitch. I heard you're going to Chiapas.
Mitch: Yeah. You've been there, haven't you, Julie?
Julie: Yes, for two weeks last summer. Do you want some tips?
Mitch: That would be great!
Julie: Well, the Miso-ha waterfall is a must-see. It's humongous! And you can walk right down to the waterfall and stand in a cave *behind* the water.
Mitch: Wow, I'll definitely do that.
Julie: But be careful—the path is really slippery.
Mitch: OK, thanks.
Julie: And there's another waterfall, too: Agua Azul. You have to go swimming there. The water is so clear and beautiful. It's absolutely breathtaking!
Mitch: But isn't the undertow too strong to swim?
Julie: No, everyone goes swimming there.
Mitch: I guess I was thinking of somewhere else. But it sounds like it's worth seeing.
Julie: You also shouldn't miss the pyramids at Palenque. But don't go in the morning. It's often too foggy to see everything well.
Mitch: Foggy?
Julie: Yes. The ruins of this ancient city are in a valley in the middle of a jungle. Oh, and it's worth going to Sumidero Canyon, too. Take a boat tour of the river at the bottom of the canyon. The scenery is spectacular with canyon walls that are a thousand meters high and covered with lush vegetation.
Mitch: Thanks for your help. Everything sounds great!

REVIEW TEST 2 (UNITS 6–10)

Example: **A:** Why do people traditionally throw a bouquet of flowers at a wedding ceremony?
B: It's the custom. People believe that the woman who catches the bouquet will be the next one to get married.

1. **A:** Hey, Megan. How are you?
   B: Great. I just graduated from law school. I decided not to go to medical school after all.
   A: Well, congratulations!

2. **A:** Have you seen the new electric car from Yakota?
   B: Yeah, it's really innovative. If I needed a new car, I'd definitely buy one.

3. **A:** I didn't know you were going to buy a computer.
   B: We wouldn't have bought it if it hadn't been such a great price.

4. **A:** They should encourage tourism on this island. It would bring in a lot of money.
   B: True, but buildings and more people could have a negative impact on the island.

Elizabeth: Hi, Sarah.
Sarah: Hi, Elizabeth. Do you mind if I ask you a question?
Elizabeth: Absolutely not. What's up?
Sarah: I'm not sure about the customs here for Independence Day. I'm going on a picnic, and everyone's taking something. I was going to take soda, but I decided to take something else. It's OK if I take sandwiches, isn't it?
Elizabeth: Absolutely perfect.
Sarah: So how else do you celebrate the holiday?
Elizabeth: Well, there's a parade. And at night they set off fireworks. You're going to watch them, aren't you?
Sarah: Definitely. Thanks for your help!

A: Who do you want to win the election?
B: The Yellow Party.
A: The Yellow Party? But they want to make so many changes. They want to spend less money to fight terrorism.
B: Yes, but they want to use that money to fight poverty. I think that's more important.
A: I'm afraid I don't agree. The nation needs protection from terrorists.
B: Terrorism *is* very dangerous, but I think poverty is a bigger problem, no matter what. We have to help the people who need it most. It's time for change.
A: I guess we'll have to agree to disagree!

Answer Key

Note: "Sample response" indicates a sample of what students may produce. Answers will vary. Sample responses throughout the tests do not necessarily indicate the "correct" response.

UNIT 1

1. customary
2. before
3. taboo
4. title and last name
5. punctuality
6. taught a class
7. offensive
8. taboo
9. customary
10. table manners
11. etiquette
12. aren't you
13. am I
14. doesn't he
15. haven't they
16. did they
17. 2 She left Spain.   1 She learned Spanish pretty well.
18. 1 He heard the news.   2 His boss told him about the promotion.
19. 2 We arrived at the office.   1 The meeting started.
20. hadn't yet bought
21. had already begun
22. had already started
23. d
24. a
25. c
26. true
27. false
28. true
29. false
30. true

31–33.
- *(Sample response:)* Tuesday morning was unbelievably busy. By 10, I had already been to the doctor for my checkup and gone food shopping. And then I had to go to work at 11. When I got to work, I hadn't eaten yet. So I got a snack on my break.
- *(Sample response:)* The etiquette in my country has gone through a lot of changes in the last twenty-five years. Since technology has increased, we communicate with many people from all over. This has increased the cultural literacy in my country. People are more aware of what is customary in other cultures and what is taboo.

UNIT 2

1. a
2. c
3. d
4. false
5. false
6. true
7. cough medicine
8. painkiller
9. antacid
10. must
11. might/may
12. must
13. might/may
14. She feels like she's going to vomit.
15. Thanks for giving me an appointment.
16. I need help immediately.
17. The medication can make you feel nauseous.
18. **b.** a checkup
19. **a.** a conventional doctor
20. **a.** my gums are swollen
21. **b.** an X-ray
22. **c.** Spiritual healing
23. *(Sample response:)* You must have allergies.
24. *(Sample response:)* It must really hurt.
25. *(Sample response:)* You must be so happy!
26. Laughter can help your body fight disease.
27. If you need to lower your blood pressure, laughing might help.
28. Laughter is one form of exercise.
29. Laughing keeps your brain healthy so you can remember more.
30. Laughter is one good way to improve your health.

31–33.
- *(Sample response:)* I have always used conventional medicine. I usually like it because it makes me better when I'm sick. But one thing I don't like is that doctors always want to give me a prescription. Sometimes I think people could try to heal themselves other ways.
- *(Sample response:)*
   1. Me: Could you recommend a doctor? I'm sick.
      Friend: There's one not far from here. Her name is Dr. Melendez.
   2. Me: Hello. I wonder if I might be able to see the doctor today. I'm sick.
      Receptionist: Let me check. Could you be here by 2:15?
   3. Receptionist: You must be Nicole. You're here to see Dr. Melendez, aren't you?
      Me: That's right. I've been feeling sick.
   4. Me: My stomach is killing me.
      Doctor: That must hurt. Let's have a look. I think it's a good idea to take an antacid.
      Me: Are there any side effects?

UNIT 3

1. reliable
2. copying
3. fast
4. auto repair
5. helpful
6. tailoring

AK1

Answer Key (continued)

7. reasonable
8. go
9. plan
10. framed
11. finished
12. pay
13. Can you make her sign the forms
14. You can have the package delivered tomorrow morning
15. They're having the apartment cleaned before the party
16. She'll get someone to call the restaurant for a reservation
17. The store manager will have a sign printed to announce the sale
18. i
19. f
20. e
21. g
22. a
23. Annie wants to have (OR get) her skirt lengthened
24. Harry wants to have (OR get) his suit dry-cleaned
25. Irene wants to have (OR get) her shoes repaired
26. i
27. a
28. f
29. d
30. c

31–33.
- *(Sample response:)* I'm planning a party for my mom's birthday. I'm going to have a chef make the food so we don't have to cook. I'll have my sister be in charge of the decorations because she's very creative. I'm going to have the invitations printed at a copying place. I will get one of my friends to do the music.
- *(Sample response:)* I get my hair cut at Dawn's Salon. It's a little expensive, but the quality is high. Dawn is also very honest—she never tries to get me to have anything done that I don't want. She's also very helpful when I need ideas for a new hairstyle.

UNIT 4

1. science fiction
2. autobiography
3. romance novel
4. biography
5. travel book
6. thriller
7. short stories
8. **b.** read articles online
9. **c.** read aloud to him
10. **b.** cliff-hanger
11. **b.** skim through them
12. **c.** fast read
13. I was surprised that he wrote another book.
14. Do you know where Tina left the magazine?
15. I wonder if she liked the movie.
16. Did he like the food? I guess not.
17. I'd like to know whose jacket this is.
18. Tell me what the novel's about.
19. I don't know if we'll be late, but I hope not.

20. if (OR whether) the Book Barn had a sale on paperbacks last week
21. if (OR whether) they sell newspapers at the little store down the street
22. where you found the article about low-calorie desserts
23. why more people read comics in Japan than in Brazil
24. false
25. false
26. false
27. true
28. *(Sample response:)* when the new library is going to open
29. *(Sample response:)* whether more people get their news from the television or newspapers
30. *(Sample response:)* why novels about police officers are so popular

31–33.
- *(Sample response:)* I love to read novels. I can't get enough of them. For me, it's very relaxing to curl up with a novel and get involved in the story. I prefer fiction because I think it's more entertaining than nonfiction.
- *(Sample response:)* I usually read in my living room because it has a lot of sunlight. I really don't enjoy reading on the train or in other public places. I need a quiet space to read. Besides books, I often skim through magazines and newspapers, and I enjoy doing the puzzles.

UNIT 5

1. flood
2. catastrophic
3. not known
4. are no deaths
5. in a first-aid kit
6. e
7. b
8. g
9. f
10. true
11. false
12. true
13. false
14. Dad said (that) the batteries in the flashlight needed to be changed.
15. The weather forecaster said (that) it was the worst storm in fifty years.
16. The mayor of the town said to evacuate immediately.
17. The doctor told them (that) it was important to get vaccinations before their trip.
18. The TV reporter said (that) thousands of people had been affected by the flood.
19. The emergency workers said not to leave our homes yet.
20. say
21. say
22. tell
23. say
24. no
25. yes
26. no
27. no information

Answer Key (continued)

28. *(Sample response:)* that I talked too much
29. *(Sample response:)* not to shop at Farmerton Market
30. *(Sample response:)* that a police officer had saved a family of four

31–33.
- *(Sample response:)* Sometimes there is a flood when it rains a lot. Floods can happen during storms such as hurricanes, typhoons, and monsoons because they bring a lot of rain. The water can cause property damage, and it can be dangerous. Floods can cause a lot of destruction and leave many people homeless.
- *(Sample response:)* People can prepare for an emergency in several ways. They should have flashlights because there might be a power outage. A radio with batteries can be useful, too. It's a good idea to have some non-perishable food, like food in cans, and extra drinking water in bottles. A first-aid kit can be useful if anyone gets hurt.

REVIEW TEST 1 (UNITS 1–5)

1. false
2. false
3. true
4. false
5. must be able to deliver
6. was really good
7. were not helpful
8. false
9. false
10. true
11. false
12. true
13. Can you fill in for me? I have a pain in my chest.
14. She's getting her hair washed.
15. The storm might cause a flood.
16. He may be stuck in traffic.
17. **b.** had filled
18. **b.** aren't I
19. **c.** must not be
20. **c.** will be able to
21. **b.** we arrived
22. **a.** to eat
23. **b.** cleaned
24. **c.** to give
25. **a.** that
26. **b.** to prepare
27. **a.** that I got
28. **a.** say
29. **b.** not to
30. by their clothing
31. appointment
32. power outage
33. severe
34. mild
35. get antacids
36. Yes, it really is.
37. I'll see what I can do.
38. Yes, a small gift is nice.
39. It's a novel.
40. Please call me Russell.
41. At the newsstand around the corner.
42. *(Sample response:)* I had gone to Miami twice before I was 15 years old.
43. *(Sample response:)* I might get my dress dry-cleaned for a social event.
44. *(Sample response:)* You know where I live, don't you?
45. *(Sample response:)* You must be in a lot of pain.
46. *(Sample response:)* My friend told me that he found a new job.
47. yes
48. no
49. no
50. no
51. **a.** doesn't know table etiquette from
52. **c.** time and punctuality
53. **b.** usually
54. **a.** might

55–60.
- **greetings and meeting someone for the first time** *(Sample response:)* When I meet someone, I always shake their hand and say hello. Usually, I introduce myself and ask what they prefer to be called. I try to ask questions to make small talk with the other person. I may talk about the weather or occupations. I don't ask personal questions that may make the person feel uncomfortable. If I'm in another country, I might ask about proper etiquette.
- **good etiquette for males and females in your country** *(Sample response:)* It's polite for males to open doors for females, but females don't have to do the same thing. It's nice for males to pull out a chair for a woman to sit in. Men should wear suits to many offices, but women don't have to. They can wear a skirt and a blouse. Women may greet each other with a kiss on the cheek, but this is not customary for men.
- **medications you use for specific symptoms or medical problems** *(Sample response:)* I'm allergic to a lot of things. I take a decongestant every day. The doctor gives me a prescription for it. When my stomach hurts, I take an antacid. Sometimes I have to take two or three until I feel better. If I have a headache, I take some painkillers.
- **a service you've been happy or unhappy with and why** *(Sample response:)* I took my shoes to a shoe repair place, and the service was awful. My shoes weren't ready on time. It wasn't a professional job. The clerk wasn't helpful. The prices were not reasonable—I paid too much! The shoe repair place is not reliable, and I won't take anything there again.
- **an emergency, severe weather event, or natural disaster** *(Sample response:)* Earthquakes can be very severe natural disasters. They often cause a lot of destruction, and they can have a large economic impact. They can leave people homeless, without any shelter. Often the death toll from an earthquake can be very high. People who live in areas with frequent earthquakes should keep emergency supplies in their homes. These include bottles of water, non-perishable food, flashlights, and a first-aid kit.

Answer Key (continued)

- **reading and literature in your country** *(Sample response:)* Comics are very popular in my country. I don't really like them, but I don't think they are trash. I think that any book is good, because you can always learn something from it. I think that more people read magazines and comics than books. But people should read more books because there are some authors from my country that are very good. And also there are a lot of translations of books from other places.

SPEAKING TEST 1 (UNITS 1–5)

(Possible responses; accept other meaningful responses. See scoring guidelines on page iv.)

1. The service at this office must be helpful and professional.
2. [man] I wonder if I might be able to see the dentist today.
   [receptionist] Luckily, there was a cancellation today. Could you be here by 1:00?
   [man] That's fine. Thank you.
3. [woman 1] This is a nice office, isn't it?
   [woman 2] Yes, it really is.
4. He must have a toothache.
5. The dentist's office looks nice, but there are a lot of people waiting. The dentist must be slow. [referring to man on the other end of the phone] He's making an appointment to see the dentist. [referring to 2 women talking] They are making small talk and getting to know each other. [referring to man holding his mouth] He has a dental emergency. His tooth is killing him. [referring to sign on reception desk] May 6 is a day that the office is closed. It must be an important holiday.

6–10. Answers to personal questions will vary.

UNIT 6

1. no
2. yes
3. no
4. She didn't pass the exam.
5. Her tastes changed.
6. Her parents talked her out of it.
7. She changed her mind.
8. was going to
9. were going to
10. were going to
11. was going to
12. f
13. e
14. b
15. d
16. **b.** shouldn't have spent
17. **a.** may have left
18. **a.** could have taken
19. **a.** must have forgotten
20. **c.** might have been
21. **c.** must have been
22. a
23. e
24. d
25. **a.** should
26. **b.** must
27. **a.** can do the job
28. *(Sample response:)* I shouldn't have left school before I finished.
29. *(Sample response:)* I have good mathematical ability.
30. *(Sample response:)* I thought I would be a doctor.

31–33.
- *(Sample response:)* I want to be a nurse. A nurse has to be patient and like to help people. I'm caring and patient. I really enjoy helping people and taking care of them.
- *(Sample response:)* I should have studied art. I think I would have been very happy. But, I may not have been able to make a living as an artist. I didn't choose to study art, though, so I must not have been very interested in it.

UNIT 7

1. g
2. d
3. a
4. h
5. b
6. f
7. c
8. f
9. g
10. d
11. b
12. c

Note to teacher: For items 13–17, assign 1 point for each correctly underlined adjective clause; 1 point for each correctly circled relative pronoun; and 1 point for each correctly placed arrow.

13. Rosh Hashana is a religious holiday (that) celebrates the Jewish new year.
14. Valentine's Day is a great holiday for people (who) are in love.
15. The fireworks (that) are on the 4th of July are fantastic!
16. On December 26, Boxing Day is celebrated by people (who) live in Canada.
17. Anyone (who) wears a costume can participate in the Halloween parade.
18. I; They are the couple who ~~they~~ were married on the beach yesterday.
19. C
20. I; Anyone *who (that)* wants to see the fireworks can go to the lake and watch them.
21. C
22. I; The cancan is a traditional dance that ~~X~~ comes from France.
23. the town square
24. involving a large group of people
25. accepted
26. have to
27. Throwing
28. *(Sample response:)* Independence Day; is celebrated with picnics, fireworks, and parades

Answer Key (continued)

29. (Sample response:) Parades; like music
30. (Sample response:) are celebrated by the whole family together

31–33.
- (Sample response:) Most weddings in my country are very formal. The bride usually wears a long dress, and it's almost always white. The groom usually wears a tuxedo or a suit. It's considered bad luck for the groom to see the bride on their wedding day before the time of the ceremony, so most couples spend their wedding day apart.
- (Sample response:) My favorite holiday is The Day of the Dead. It is a religious holiday. People may visit graves of close relatives, have picnics, and tell stories to remember the dead. They also make and share sugary candy shaped like animals or skulls.

UNIT 8

1. didn't win
2. rained
3. keep
4. can win
5. unique
6. get lost
7. would have heard
8. took
9. decide
10. doesn't/does not rain
11. unique/usual/normal/customary
12. high-tech/state-of-the-art/inefficient/cutting-edge
13. top-of-the-line/first-rate/high-end/low-tech
14. old-fashioned/revolutionary/novel/new
15. efficient
16. state-of-the-art
17. wacky
18. top-of-the-line
19. false
20. false
21. true
22. would have had their own
23. the toothbrush was the most important invention
24. they wouldn't have clean teeth
25. b. No harm done
26. c. If you use it, bugs won't go near you
27. a. I had tons of calls
28. (Sample response:) the weather is good
29. (Sample response:) will go to the beach and relax
30. (Sample response:) would get a fast motorcycle

31–33.
- (Sample response:) When I was five years old, I started to take swimming classes. I loved them, and I continued with them until I graduated from high school. I got a lot of confidence from swimming. If I hadn't started swimming, I wouldn't have been so confident in myself.

- (Sample response:) The cell phone is important to me. My life would have been different if the cell phone hadn't been invented. It has had a big impact on me—I don't go anywhere without it. Even though I don't have a top-of-the-line cell phone, it's still a high-tech invention that I find very useful.

UNIT 9

1. true
2. false
3. false
4. false
5. true
6. conservative
7. moderate
8. liberal
9. radical
10. poverty
11. education
12. health
13. advice
14. progress
15. The new program encourages young people to participate in government.
16. Many groups urge people to vote.
17. The dictator doesn't allow anyone to speak against him.
18. The king appears to be in control of the government.
19. Several organizations offered to help after the disaster.
20. b. The woman is against smoking indoors.
21. b. People aren't permitted to read certain things.
22. c. They are debating the issue.
23. work together
24. local and global issues
25. are
26. disasters
27. can learn
28. (Sample response:) elections; then people can choose their own leaders and decision-makers
29. (Sample response:) capital punishment; people don't have the right to decide when another person should die, for any reason
30. (Sample response:) compulsory military service; your country might need you to fight in an emergency

31–33.
- (Sample response:) Poverty is a global problem that concerns me. Since poverty also leads to starvation and infectious disease, something should be done to stop it. Governments should establish programs to give people jobs and feed the children. If more people worked harder, this wouldn't be such a big problem.
- (Sample response:) I am a moderate. I don't like the government to have too much control in people's lives, but I think that sometimes the government has to be involved, especially to help people. For example, I think that it's the government's responsibility to help people who suffer from poverty. But I think that other organizations should also help so the government doesn't have too much power.

Answer Key (continued)

UNIT 10

1. c
2. e
3. a
4. cave
5. slippery
6. often foggy
7. has lush plant life
8. f
9. a
10. c
11. b
12. e
13. Island
14. environmentalists
15. cliffs
16. breathtaking
17. pollution
18. on
19. of
20. on, of
21. of
22. in
23. **b.** is no development
24. **a.** south of
25. **b.** not recommended
26. **b.** walk
27. **a.** don't like flying
28. *(Sample response:)* It's too cold for people to swim in the winter.
29. *(Sample response:)* It's too far for me to walk that distance.
30. *(Sample response:)* It's too early for my family to get up at that time.

31–33.
- *(Sample response:)* Today Nancy and I climbed to the top of Mt. Helen. It was exhausting. The path was really steep, and it was rocky and dangerous. But it was worth it. The view from the top of the mountain was spectacular! There was a lush valley at the bottom of the mountain. It's definitely a must-see.
- *(Sample response:)* There are many things I can do in my community to help curb global warming. I can take public transportation or ride my bike to work and school instead of driving. I can take shorter showers and use less hot water. I can recycle old paper, glass, and metal. Also, I can talk to local lawmakers about my interest in curbing global warming, and I can support the actions they take to help curb global warming, too.

REVIEW TEST 2 (UNITS 6–10)

1. **c.** changed her mind
2. **a.** doesn't need
3. **a.** because it was
4. **b.** an environmentalist
5. go on a picnic
6. thought she would
7. changed her mind
8. parade
9. fireworks
10. liberal
11. poverty
12. disagrees with
13. doesn't agree
14. She must have forgotten her umbrella.
15. The family got together for the holiday.
16. They just got married.
17. It's really foggy. He must have gotten lost.
18. tailor
19. urgent
20. politics
21. puzzles
22. tornado
23. slippery
24. a democracy
25. an island
26. **a.** to bring
27. **c.** was going to see
28. **a.** that is celebrated
29. **b.** would improve
30. **a.** who has
31. **c.** studied
32. **a.** hadn't had
33. **c.** Health
34. **a.** all passengers to have
35. **c.** have avoided
36. **a.** for people to swim in
37. **c.** on
38. **a.** too steep for us to climb
39. **b.** my friends to write
40. It's too spectacular to miss.
    You'd better not miss it.
41. Would you say that's a touchy question?
    Do you think that's too personal?
42. I just won't hear of it.
    I refuse to do it.
43. I couldn't agree more.
    I couldn't have said it better myself.
44. **c.** think about education and literacy
45. **c.** can be enjoyed by adults and children
46. **b.** working in your own neighborhood
47. **c.** might want to participate in a literacy project
48. **c.** give gifts
49. *(Sample response:)* study law, but I changed my mind
50. *(Sample response:)* I would buy a new car
51. *(Sample response:)* (that) you wanted to be a dancer
52. *(Sample response:)* I would enjoy going to the movies more
53. *(Sample response:)* to vote and participate in government
54. *(Sample response:)* studied for my exam

Answer Key (continued)

55–60.

- **a life decision that you've made** *(Sample response:)* I decided to go to college after high school. My parents tried to talk me out of it, but I went. I was going to study art, but then my tastes changed. I'm happy with my decision to go, but I should have studied engineering instead of philosophy. It's hard to make a living as a philosopher.

- **a holiday that you celebrate** *(Sample response:)* A holiday that I celebrate is Christmas. Our family gets together every year. We give each other gifts. I also send cards to family and friends. Usually, we eat too much food! We relax a lot and have fun.

- **an idea for a new invention**
  (Sample response:) I would like to invent a homework machine. You put in the assignment, and the machine does the homework for you. But I also want to be able to learn the lessons when the machine does my homework. This machine would be very high-tech. If I invented it, I think I would make a lot of money. It's such an innovative idea; I'm sure that everyone would want one.

- **your point of view on a controversial issue**
  (Sample response:) I am opposed to prohibiting smoking indoors. I don't smoke, but I think it's each person's decision whether or not to smoke inside. If I go somewhere and I don't like the smoke, then I can leave. It's not the government's job to control people's health. Some people say that prohibiting smoking indoors would protect people who work in restaurants and other places that normally allow smoking. But if they don't want to work in a place with smoke, then they can look for a job somewhere else.

- **a natural setting in your country**
  (Sample response:) Pipa Beach is one of the most breathtaking natural settings in the world. It's a beautiful beach in Northeastern Brazil. You can visit the Pipa Ecological Sanctuary, where the coastal rainforest covers ancient coastal dunes. You can see marine turtles in the bay and swim with dolphins at Ponta do Madeiro Beach.

SPEAKING TEST 2 (UNITS 6–10)

(Possible responses; accept other meaningful responses. See scoring guidelines on page iv.)

1. I was going to study math, but I decided to study law instead.
2. She wants to learn about the traditions of the holiday.
3. [Man on left]: Development helps people. It can bring money to a place that needs it.
   [Man on right]: That may be true, but it's not always good. It can affect the environment in very negative ways.
4. She is reading about a place she wants to travel to. There is a valley with a forest and a lake. There's an island in the lake. The land is mountainous and lush. There is a cave in the mountains. There is a path, too. It looks steep. It's too dangerous to walk on.
5. The two men sitting down are debating the pros and cons of environmental development; the man on the left might be a developer, and the one on the right is probably an environmentalist. The woman on the right is reading a travel book. She wants to go hiking. The woman at the computer is using the Internet. I think the Internet is the top invention in history.

6–10. Answers to personal questions will vary.

About the CD-ROM

The CD-ROM is a hybrid disk that can be used as a CD-ROM or as an audio CD.

To use as a CD-ROM (to create custom-made printed tests, using **Exam**View® *Assessment Suite*) Insert the disk into the CD-ROM drive of your computer. Follow the instructions on the CD-ROM or on page v to install the **Exam**View® test-generator software.

To use as an audio CD (to listen to the audio for all listening comprehension exercises) You can play the audio CD on any CD player or on a computer, using Windows Media Player™, iTunes™, or another media player.

System Requirements

To use the **Exam**View® *Assessment Suite*, your computer must meet or exceed the following requirements:

- 100 MB of available hard drive space
- 256 MB of available RAM (512 MB recommended)
- Monitor capable of displaying 16-bit color with 800 x 600 resolution
- Internet connection to access the test-hosting features, and for Content Update
- CD-ROM drive

Windows®
- Intel Pentium® II 120 MHz or compatible processor
- Microsoft Windows® 2000/XP/Vista

Macintosh®
- PowerPC 120 MHz or higher processor
- Mac OS X

Single User License Agreement and Limited Warranty

THESE TERMS APPLY TO ALL LICENSED SOFTWARE ON THE DISK EXCEPT THAT THE TERMS FOR USE OF ANY SHAREWARE OR FREEWARE ON THE DISKETTES ARE AS SET FORTH IN THE ELECTRONIC LICENSE LOCATED ON THE DISK:

1. **GRANT OF LICENSE and OWNERSHIP:** The enclosed computer programs ("Software") are licensed, not sold, to you by Pearson Education, Inc. ("We" or the "Company") and in consideration of your payment of the license fee, which is part of the price you paid, and your agreement to these terms. We reserve any rights not granted to you. You own only the disk(s) but we and/or our licensors own the Software itself. This license allows you to use and display your copy of the Software on a single computer (i.e., with a single CPU) at a single location, so long as you comply with the terms of this Agreement. You may make one copy for back up, or transfer your copy to another CPU, provided that the Software is usable on only one computer.

2. **RESTRICTIONS:** You may not transfer or distribute the Software or documentation to anyone else. Except for backup, you may not copy the documentation or the Software. You may not network the Software or otherwise use it on more than one computer or computer terminal at the same time. You may not reverse engineer, disassemble, decompile, modify, adapt, translate, or create derivative works based on the Software or the Documentation. You may be held legally responsible for any copying or copyright infringement which is caused by your failure to abide by the terms of these restrictions.

3. **TERMINATION:** This license is effective until terminated. This license will terminate automatically without notice from the Company if you fail to comply with any provisions or limitations of this license. Upon termination, you shall destroy the Documentation and all copies of the Software. All provisions of this Agreement as to limitation and disclaimer of warranties, limitation of liability, remedies or damages, and our ownership rights shall survive termination.

4. **LIMITED WARRANTY AND DISCLAIMER OF WARRANTY:** Company warrants that for a period of 30 days from the date you purchase this Software, the Software, when properly installed and used in accordance with the Documentation, will operate in substantial conformity with the description of the Software set forth in the Documentation, and that for a period of 30 days the disk(s) on which the Software is delivered shall be free from defects in materials and workmanship under normal use. The Company does not warrant that the Software will meet your requirements or that the operation of the Software will be uninterrupted or error-free. Your only remedy and the Company's only obligation under these limited warranties is, at the Company's option, return of the disk for a refund of any amounts paid for it by you or replacement of the disk. THIS LIMITED WARRANTY IS THE ONLY WARRANTY PROVIDED BY THE COMPANY AND ITS LICENSORS, AND THE COMPANY AND ITS LICENSORS DISCLAIM ALL OTHER WARRANTIES, EXPRESS OR IMPLIED, INCLUDING WITHOUT LIMITATION, THE IMPLIED WARRANTIES OF MERCHANTABILITY AND FITNESS FOR A PARTICULAR PURPOSE. THE COMPANY DOES NOT WARRANT, GUARANTEE OR MAKE ANY REPRESENTATION REGARDING THE ACCURACY, RELIABILITY, CURRENTNESS, USE, OR RESULTS OF USE, OF THE SOFTWARE.

5. **LIMITATION OF REMEDIES AND DAMAGES:** IN NO EVENT, SHALL THE COMPANY OR ITS EMPLOYEES, AGENTS, LICENSORS, OR CONTRACTORS BE LIABLE FOR ANY INCIDENTAL, INDIRECT, SPECIAL, OR CONSEQUENTIAL DAMAGES ARISING OUT OF OR IN CONNECTION WITH THIS LICENSE OR THE SOFTWARE, INCLUDING FOR LOSS OF USE, LOSS OF DATA, LOSS OF INCOME OR PROFIT, OR OTHER LOSSES, SUSTAINED AS A RESULT OF INJURY TO ANY PERSON, OR LOSS OF OR DAMAGE TO PROPERTY, OR CLAIMS OF THIRD PARTIES, EVEN IF THE COMPANY OR AN AUTHORIZED REPRESENTATIVE OF THE COMPANY HAS BEEN ADVISED OF THE POSSIBILITY OF SUCH DAMAGES. IN NO EVENT SHALL THE LIABILITY OF THE COMPANY FOR DAMAGES WITH RESPECT TO THE SOFTWARE EXCEED THE AMOUNTS ACTUALLY PAID BY YOU, IF ANY, FOR THE SOFTWARE OR THE ACCOMPANYING TEXTBOOK. BECAUSE SOME JURISDICTIONS DO NOT ALLOW THE LIMITATION OF LIABILITY IN CERTAIN CIRCUMSTANCES, THE ABOVE LIMITATIONS MAY NOT ALWAYS APPLY TO YOU.

6. **GENERAL:** This agreement shall be construed in accordance with the laws of the United States of America and the State of New York, applicable to contracts made in New York, and shall benefit the Company, its affiliates and assignees. This agreement is the complete and exclusive statement of the agreement between you and the Company and supersedes all proposals or prior agreements, oral, or written, and any other communications between you and the Company or any representative of the Company relating to the subject matter of this agreement. If you are a U.S. government user, this Software is licensed with "restricted rights" as set forth in subparagraphs (a)-(d) of the Commercial Computer-Restricted Rights clause at FAR 52.227-19 or in subparagraphs (c)(1)(ii) of the Rights in Technical Data and Computer Software clause at DFARS 252.227-7013, and similar clauses, as applicable. Should you have any questions concerning this agreement or if you wish to contact the Company for any reason, please contact in writing: Customer Service, Pearson Education, Inc., 10 Bank Street, White Plains, NY 10606.